The Crusading General

The Crusading General

The Life of General Sir Bernard Paget
GCB DSO MC

Julian Paget

Pen & Sword
MILITARY

First published in Great Britain in 2008 by
Pen & Sword Military
an imprint of
Pen & Sword Books Ltd
47 Church Street
Barnsley
South Yorkshire
S70 2AS

ISBN 978 18441 5810 2

A CIP catalogue record for this book is
available from the British Library.

Typeset in Palatino Linotype by
Lamorna Publishing Services.

Printed and bound in England by Biddles Ltd

Pen & Sword Books Ltd. incorporates the imprints of
Pen & Sword Aviation, Pen & Sword Maritime, Pen & Sword Military,
Wharncliffe Local History, Remember When Publications,
Pen & Sword Select, Pen & Sword Military Classics and Leo Cooper.

For a complete list of Pen & Sword titles please contact
PEN & SWORD BOOKS LIMITED
47 Church Street, Barnsley, South Yorkshire, S70 2AS, England
E-mail: enquiries@pen-and-sword.co.uk
Website: www.pen-and-sword.co.uk

Contents

Maps and Diagrams . . . .*vi*
Preface . . . .*vii*
Foreword . . . .*ix*

1. Early Years (1887-1914) 1
2. The Kaiser's War (1914-1918) 8
3. Between the Wars (1919-1939) .14
4. Norway (1940) 26
5. Home Forces (1940-1943) 44
6. Who Planned D-Day? (1942-1944) 57
7. Forging the Sword (1941-1943) 77
8. 21st Army Group (June-December 1943) 94
9. The Middle East (1944-1946) .101
10. The Greek Connection 127
11. Citizenship (1944-1948) 137
12. The Royal Hospital (1949-1957) 147
13. Retirement 154
14. The Crusader 161

Appendix A The Life of Bernard Paget 165
Appendix B Original Sources 168
Selected Bibliography 170
Index 172

Maps and Diagrams

Paget Coat of Arms xiii
Norway 27
Southern Norway 31
The Three D-Day Plans 60

Preface

The achievements of great men are part of our history, particularly if they have themselves contributed to that history. This certainly applies to my father, who played a significant part in the Second World War. But he was a man of exceptional modesty, and he firmly refused to write his own memoirs, or allow anyone else to do it. He was determined not to join 'The War of the Generals', with each setting out to promote their own claim to fame.

As a result, little has been written about his achievements, and there are gaps in the records which could and should be filled from his diaries, letters and papers, and I believe that this should now be done. This book is an attempt to fill some of those gaps, without letting it become either a biography or memoirs. My father kept a personal diary throughout the war, which provides much previously unpublished material.

This book is very much a 'broad brush' picture, with emphasis on the matters that are particularly relevant to my father, and on which he has something of interest to contribute. On this basis, four subjects are given particular prominence; the Norwegian Campaign of 1940, when he commanded the ill-fated expedition to Andalsnes; the planning of D-Day, in which he played a significant, but largely unrecognized, role; the training of 21st Army Group, which was possibly his greatest achievement; and finally, his crusade for the teaching of citizenship which is now so relevant, sixty years on.

In accordance with my father's wishes, I have tried to avoid any criticism of others, or to cause controversy. I have not sought to resolve the rights and wrongs of various controversial issues in which he was involved, but have stated the situation as seen by my father at the time, and have left it to readers to make their own judgements.

It is difficult for a son to write objectively about his father, but in my case, it is made easier, first, because my father's achievements speak for themselves, and second, because the picture is completed by the opinions of many others.

Julian Paget

Foreword
by General Sir Robert Pascoe
KCB MBE

I once spent just over an hour in the company of General Sir Bernard Paget. It was the summer of 1952 and, as a private National Service soldier and then an officer cadet at Sandhurst, I had been in the Army for less than two years. He was a General with forty years service behind him, including battle and command experience in two world wars involving him in many important decisions. Needless to say, I was somewhat overawed by the occasion.

We 'took tea' together as he interviewed me to see if I was suitable to be commissioned into the Regiment of which he was the Colonel, the Oxfordshire and Buckinghamshire Light Infantry (43rd and 52nd). I didn't think the interview went very well, and if anyone had told me then, that some fifty years later, I, as the senior surviving officer of my old Regiment, would be invited to write the Foreword in a book about his life and times, I would not have believed him!

During the Second World War Bernard Paget made a major contribution to the outcome of the war, and greatly improved the training and the reputation of the British Army. Not for nothing has he been described as the man who did more to improve the training of the British soldier than anyone since Sir John Moore in the early 1800s.

In the 43rd and 52nd we all respected General Paget as our

outstanding senior officer, but his service to the country has not been widely recognized. He was, of course, awarded many decorations and medals, he was the country's senior serving general and, in his retirement, he became Governor of The Royal Hospital, Chelsea. But few people know how close he came to leading the British Army, which he had trained so well, onto the beaches of Normandy in Operation Overlord in June 1944.

This prize command was taken from Paget's grasp and given to Montgomery, a decision which General Brooke, the CIGS, admits in his diaries caused him much anxiety at the time, because of his 'great personal admiration and affection for him'. Many a man would have been bitter and resentful at this blow, but Paget never expressed his disappointment, and got on with the alternative job he was given in the Middle East.

After the war, Paget decided not to publish any diary or memoir, and deliberately avoided the 'word games' entered into by many of his contemporaries. Now, in this book, Julian Paget, with unique access to his father's papers and diaries, and several military history books already published, sets out for us a clear picture of a great man, which, while doing justice to his father's career, does not betray the latter's determination to avoid raising issues that he thought were best left alone. He does military historians a great service by throwing light on his father's experiences and opinions during many momentous years.

This is an interesting and revealing account of a professional soldier's career, and his views during a critical time in our nation's history. It also shows Bernard Paget in a light which does him the full credit to which he was justly entitled.

Robert Pascoe.

Late The Oxfordshire and Buckinghamshire Light Infantry
(43rd and 52nd) and The Royal Green Jackets

The Armorial Bearings of
General Sir Bernard Charles Tolver Paget, G.C.B., D.S.O., M.C.

College of Arms
MCMLVII.

G. R. Bellew,
Garter King of Arms.

Chapter 1

Early Years (1887-1914)

I'm going to be a soldier too.
                                    (Bernard, aged 12)

It was June 1899, and Oxford University was preparing for the ancient ceremony of Encaenia, when honorary degrees are conferred on outstanding national figures. The Dean of Christ Church, one of the leading Oxford colleges, was my grandfather, Francis Paget, and he had some very distinguished guests staying with him at the Deanery for the occasion. They were headed by the Duke and Duchess of York (the future King George V and Queen Mary), and with them was Field Marshal Lord Kitchener, Commander-in-Chief of the British Army and a national hero.

The Dean introduced his son, Bernard,[1] aged 12 to the Field Marshal, and the boy showed particular interest in the great man's medals. After a good look, he announced 'I'm going to be a soldier too'. And indeed, he kept his word, ending his career as General Sir Bernard Paget, GCB DSO MC ADC DL, Commander-in-Chief Home Forces (1941-1944) and Commander-in-Chief Middle East (1944-1946). He was the longest serving C.-in-C. in the Second World War, and became the senior General in the British Army.

Soldiering was always in Bernard's mind, and his three brothers recalled that in mock battles in the Deanery garden it was always Bernard who took command. He was the fourth child and third son of Francis Paget and his wife, Helen, and was followed by a sister and another brother, making a family of six. They lived first in the Canon's House at Christ Church and then in the Deanery next door from 1891 to 1901, when Bernard's father was appointed Bishop of Oxford, and they moved to the Bishop's Palace at Cuddesdon, eight miles outside Oxford. This meant that Bernard was brought up almost entirely in an exclusively ecclesiastical setting, and this undoubtedly had a strong influence on him.

His mother, Helen, was the eldest daughter of the Reverend Richard Church (1815-1890), who was Dean of St Paul's (1871-1890). A strikingly good-looking woman with vivid, auburn hair and calm, serene manner, she was an active, vital person who loved an outdoor life; she was a strong character with a mind of her own and high moral principles, which she undoubtedly handed on to all her children. She had a twin sister, Mary, who would also have a considerable influence on Bernard's life.

The Church family came from the City of Cork in Ireland, and Helen's grandfather, John Church, was a Hereditary Freeman of the City, an honour that was, in 1947, granted to Bernard, in recognition of his wartime achievements. Honorary though it was, it gave him great pleasure to be entitled to it, and he wrote to the Mayor to say so. Having said first how much he appreciated the honour, he then inquired, with his tongue well up his cheek, whether it might perhaps entitle him to some free fishing on the famous River Blackwater. But the Mayor also had a sense of humour, and replied 'Dear General, I am sure you will agree, the honour is enough'.

Bernard's family came originally from Norfolk, where they had been gentry in Great Yarmouth[2] since about 1600. His father, Francis, was the second son of six children of Sir James Paget (1814-1899), a distinguished surgeon, who became Surgeon Extraordinary to Queen Victoria and was created a Baronet in 1871. In the next generation there was a strong ecclesiastical element in the family, with two of Sir James's sons becoming Bishops, and one grandson, Bernard's elder brother Edward, becoming an Archbishop.[3]

Bernard was particularly close to his younger brother, Humphrey, born in 1891. They grew up together often sharing a room; they both joined the Army, and for most of the First World

2

War they fought in the same infantry brigade, although in different regiments.

Life in the Deanery

The ten years spent in the Deanery at Christ Church[4] were austere and routine. As was the custom in those days, there was a succession of nannies and governesses who looked after the children, but their mother kept a close eye on their upbringing. It was a rather gloomy house with no electricity and only gas lamps. Discipline was strict, and everyone had to be exceptionally well-behaved, because they were the children of the Dean, which they found decidedly irksome. They were required not only to attend Church every Sunday, but also had to learn by heart every day the Collect for the Day, as well as singing hymns round the piano at home every evening. On top of this, there were Family Prayers twice a day.

Conversation at meals was serious and subdued, and often well above the heads of the young; when there was anything that was considered unsuitable for their ears, it was said in French.

Bernard's mother died in 1900 of pneumonia, aged only 42, but happily for the six children, her twin sister, Mary Church moved in as a wonderful foster-mother, and took over their upbringing. She was also a great support to their father, which was a bonus indeed, for in June 1901 he was appointed Bishop of Oxford, which involved moving to the Bishop's Palace at Cuddesdon, and also a very heavy workload. It was an exceptionally large diocese, covering Oxfordshire, Buckinghamshire and Berkshire, which meant that it included Windsor, and he, therefore, became Chancellor of the Order of the Garter.

Cuddesdon (1901-1911)

The Bishop's Palace was a 200-year-old mansion and was even more austere and religious than Christ Church, with Family Prayers twice a day at 0845 and 2200. There were few parties, no frivolities and little social life. But the boys made the most of life in the country, riding and bicycling round the district, fishing and exploring. Army manoeuvres occasionally took place nearby at Tring, and Bernard and Humphrey used to follow the troops all day on bicycles, with Bernard showing a particular interest.

In 1886, Bernard was sent to Summerfields, a prep school in Oxford, but he did not enjoy it very much. Indeed when Humphrey contracted whooping cough, Bernard deliberately got it from him, and the two of them spent two happy weeks away from school, fishing and ferreting.

Bernard was already showing notable powers of leadership, and indeed used to issue orders to his brothers and sisters to such an extent that Aunt Mary once wrote of 'Bernard's unwarranted assumption of authority', and often felt obliged to exclaim 'Bernard dear. If I want the children admonished, I will do it myself'.

In 1901, Bernard went to Shrewsbury, where he did not distinguish himself academically, but proved a good long distance runner. In 1906 he passed into Sandhurst, and so set off on the first step of a lifetime in the Army.

It was very much his chosen career, and he was well prepared for it. He was accustomed to a simple, fairly austere life, and had been brought up to put Service before Self and to have a high sense of Duty. The making of money had never been a feature of life at home, and it never would be for him in the future. His religious faith was strong and he was, above all, a man of outstanding integrity and honesty. Indeed, his characteristics were remarkably like those of a knight setting off on the Crusades.

Looking back many years later, Bernard said of his childhood:

There is very little that I would change in my life, though I should have liked to escape from the cramping influence of Christ Church and Summerfields in my childhood.

Early Soldiering

Bernard enjoyed his time at Sandhurst, and found himself well suited to the military way of life; he did well, but was perhaps best known as a long distance runner, winning both the mile and the two mile on the same day against Woolwich.

On 18 November 1907 he passed out and was commissioned into the Oxfordshire Light Infantry, an obvious choice in view of his connections with that county. Initially he was posted to its 2nd Battalion, known as 'the 52nd', and he joined the Regiment at Tidworth. He soon applied, however, to serve abroad, partly because it would be more interesting and exciting, but also because he did not have much money, and it would be cheaper overseas.

He transferred therefore from the '52nd' to the '43rd', the overseas 1st Battalion of the Oxfordshire Light Infantry, who were stationed in India. He sailed on 5 February 1908 aboard the troopship *Plassey*, and joined the battalion at Lucknow[5]; he thoroughly enjoyed the life there, and made the most of it, playing polo, going big-game hunting and travelling whenever he could.

On 2 August 1911 his father died, aged only 60, and Bernard felt it deeply. He had always had a very close relationship with his father, and he wrote later:

> Father's friendship has been one of the greatest help of my life. All the time I have been in India, he has missed only about six (weekly) mails, in spite of his rush of work. And then, after a life of work, such as few other men have done, he died in harness, which I think is what he would have wished.

This capacity for hard work, combined with great persistence as a letter writer, were two characteristics that Bernard would inherit. He punctiliously replied to all letters, within 48 hours if at all possible, and was renowned for driving himself, and others, to the absolute limit.

Bernard had from the start been hard-up, and when his father died, he had only his Army pay to live on. He cut down on his expenses in the Mess, and tried to boost his income by serving in remote stations, and by breeding polo ponies. He had, in February 1911, qualified as an Instructor at the School of Musketry, which increased his pay, and he even considered taking up flying and joining the better-paid Flying Corps, but this did not materialize. Somehow, he survived.

When his brother Humphrey joined the Army, Bernard wrote to him somewhat pontifically, but with sincerity: 'One thing I warn you against, very specially, is on no account whatever to get into debt or borrow money'. It was a rule that he himself would always follow, refusing ever to incur a mortgage or an overdraft, and aiming to pay all bills within 24 hours! Times have changed!

He also wrote home about the possibility of war:

I have been trying to impress on my NCOs the importance now, more than ever before, of being ready, so that, having learnt as far as we can all that peace manoeuvres and text books can teach us, we may go, with a clear conscience, knowing that we have done our best, at 24 hours notice, to put our knowledge to the test of war. I hope I'm not an alarmist, but I side wholly with Lord Roberts – who wrote me a ripping letter last mail about Father and my future. One only has to read the papers to see how far we are from the millennium of peace.

In the summer of 1914 Bernard came home to England on leave, and, on 5 August, the day after war was declared, he received orders to rejoin his Regiment in India; but this was cancelled four days later, and he was appointed Captain and Adjutant of the 5th (Service) Battalion stationed at Aldershot.

Four days later Humphrey was commissioned into the 11th (Service) Battalion of The King's (Liverpool) Regiment, and by happy chance, his battalion and Bernard's were both part of the same division, the 14th Light Division. So it was that the two brothers served together for almost the entire war in the same division, and for some of the time were even in the same brigade.

Bernard promptly wrote further instructions to Humphrey, based on his authority not only as a Regular Army officer but also as an elder brother, and they are very much in character, as well as showing much of his philosophy as a soldier:

Join in uniform, but you needn't wear a sword, except on parade or as Orderly Officer, but you must wear a belt. To sum up:

a. Scrupulous punctuality.
b. Scrupulous fairness and firmness in your dealings with the men.
c. Strict obedience on your part to all orders.
d. Exact strict obedience from those under you.
e. Common sense will make you into a good Regimental officer.

Bernard remained at Aldershot with his Battalion for the next nine months, and it was May 1915 before they went to France to join the bitter fighting on the Western Front.

Notes
1. He was born at Christ Church on 15 September 1887.
2. The District Hospital in Great Yarmouth today is called The James Paget Hospital in his honour.
3. Francis, Bishop of Oxford (1901-1911), Luke, Bishop of Chester (1919-1932), Edward, Bishop of Southern Rhodesia (1925-1955), Archbishop of Central Africa (1955-1957).
4. In the garden of the Deanery there was a large chestnut tree, and under it a student from Christ Church called C.I. Dodgson (better known as Lewis Caroll) used to sit with one of the daughters of Dean Liddell (the predecessor of Dean Paget) and tell her stories about a little girl called Alice and her adventures in Wonderland.
5. Later that year both Battalions underwent a change of name, and became 1st and 2nd Battalions of the Oxfordshire and Buckinghamshire Light Infantry.

Chapter 2

The Kaiser's War (1914-1918)

The terrible slaughter of the Kaiser's War must never be allowed to happen again.

Bernard Paget

Bernard's battalion crossed to France on 20 May 1915 as part of 42 Infantry Brigade, and he soon had his first experience of being shot at – but it was by his own men, because he had not warned them that he was going out alone into No Man's Land. Luckily they missed, and he wrote in his diary:

I was interested to discover that I had no feeling of fear while being shot at and I could think quite coolly – an interesting bit of human nature. The anticipation of trouble is by far the worst sensation one has to deal with.

The 14th Light Division, of which 42 Brigade was part, was a New Army division, and was the first New Army formation to be in contact with the Germans in 1915. They started with nine months unbroken service at the front, and by the end of the first routine tour of six weeks' duty in the trenches, Bernard's battalion had lost one third of its strength. This was in fact the 'normal' rate of wastage in a so-called 'quiet' period in the Ypres Salient, where they were; they would now spend seventeen months in that sector.

On 25 September 1915 the battalion took part in the Battle of Loos. They went in with a strength of 17 officers and 767 men, and returned with 2 and 180; the two officers who survived

were the Commanding Officer[1] and Bernard, his Adjutant, who
wrote:

It is an awful grief to have lost the battalion one has seen
grow up from infancy into the splendid fighting unit which
it was two days ago, and I hardly know how to face
beginning again with new officers and new men. But that is
war.

On 30 September Bernard took over temporary command of the
Battalion while the Commanding Officer was on leave, and then
in October he went on leave himself, but did not particularly
enjoy it:

I felt at times horribly depressed and restless. The truth is
that an Adjutant ought not to take leave. I felt worried about
the Battalion all the while, and I am thankful to be going
back to it.

On 25 October, 'the cursed Hun'[2] exploded a huge mine under
the Battalion's frontline, causing 100 casualties, and then
launched an assault. Bernard organized a successful counterat-
tack, and was awarded an immediate Military Cross for his
leadership at that moment, and also for his 'conspicuous
coolness and energy throughout the campaign in France'. He
had already been twice Mentioned in Dispatches.

On 20 November he left the Battalion to become Brigade Major
at Headquarters 42 Brigade, and the Battalion Diary recorded:

His work as Adjutant with the Battalion was beyond praise;
untiring under most difficult circumstances, he was always
a model for those who worked with or under him.

In February 1916 the Battalion moved to Arras, another suppos-
edly 'quiet' sector, and on 19 July Bernard was recommended
for a Brevet Majority, which was a great tribute. He was also
offered command of a battalion in another brigade, but
declined, because he wanted to stay with his own Regiment.

On 15 February 1916 came a happy moment when Humphrey
was sent as Assistant Brigade Major to Bernard in 42 Brigade,

and the two enjoyed going out together on recces in No Man's Land.

On 11 March Bernard had another narrow escape when a 5.9-inch shell burst ten yards from him in Ronville, and he got a splinter in his arm. He was knocked out, and a nearby sentry thought he was dead – only to find himself being sharply reprimanded for not saluting! Bernard tried to avoid reporting to the Medical Officer, but the wound would not heal, and he finally had to report sick; whereupon he was in turn severely reprimanded by the MO!

On 14 April came the news that his brother, Edward, having won a MC as a Chaplain with the South African Force, had been declared 'unfit for further military service', due to heart trouble. He continued however to serve the Church in South Africa, and ended up as an Archbishop.

During April Bernard was heavily involved in the planning for the Battle of Arras, and it was about this time that he recorded in his diary the first of many subsequent criticisms of the stereotyped tactics of attack, that were the accepted doctrine of the day:

> It is time we altered our method of attack. At present, we advance in a straight line behind the barrage, irrespective of the ground, when we should be making use of the ground and cover, with room to manoeuvre in the face of the enemy.

It was something that he would put right twenty-five years later, with the introduction of Battle Drill.

On 8 May he was slightly gassed by 'some beastly Bosche [sic] shell', but fortunately suffered no long-term effects. On the same day he wrote in his diary:

> I dare say I shall look back to the present as one of the happiest times of my life, having Humphrey here with me, and an absolute top-hole General (Dudgeon).
>
> Moreover I have been so long at the job of Brigade Major that it all comes very easily to me now… In two years of active service the Brigade has suffered casualties at the rate

of 346.5 per month or 11.4 per day, a total of 322 officers and 7,993 Other Ranks.

On 24 May he wrote home:

As a nation we are an extraordinary mixture of good and bad; the men out here are the cream of the race, their relatives at home such selfish, narrow-minded creatures. People at home don't seem to realize there is a war on.

On 9 June he hitched a lift back home on leave by air:

Flew from Lympne to St Omer in a 275 hp 12 cylinder Rolls Royce de Havilland 4, with a maximum speed of 115 mph and a maximum height of 6,300 feet. We flew mostly at about 90 mph at 5,300 feet. The trip took 40 minutes.

He then picked up a staff car, and 'travelled 36 miles at 40 mph – much more exciting than flying!'

By the time of the Third Battle of Ypres in the autumn of 1916, he was beginning to feel the strain, and wrote home:

I have never felt the strain of a battle so badly as I have this time…this is my sixth battle, and one doesn't get any fresher as the war goes on.

On 10 September he wrote:

I had a very tempting offer of a job at home last week, Chief Musketry Instructor at the Commanding Officer's School at Aldershot, with the rank of Lt Colonel. But I refused it, as I did not consider that I was justified in accepting a job at home which could probably by filled by an equally good but less fit man. Moreover I am soon to get promotion to the Staff of the Division.

Sure enough, on 30 September he was appointed as GSO II to 62nd Division, commanded by Major General W.P. Braithwaite, and on 2 October he said goodbye to 42 Brigade in which he had served since landing in France in May 1915. He remained in his new job for only two months however, before being recommended for GSO II at GHQ First Echelon. His Division did not want to lose him, but he was ordered to go, and duly joined GHQ on 26 December 1917; his immediate boss was Colonel John Dill[3] under whom would serve again in the Second World War, and for whom he had a great admiration.

He did not like life at GHQ:

> …it is a soulless sort of place after a Brigade or Division. One may get more comfort, but one loses a great deal of the colour of life, and the pleasure of friends and freedom of talk.

In the New Year's Honours List of 1917 Bernard was awarded a long-deferred DSO for his work as Brigade Major at 42 Brigade

On 7 February 1918 he was home on leave and got married to his first cousin, Winifred Paget, daughter of Sir John Paget QC. They lived at first at 28 Trevor Square, and their first son, Julian, was born there on 11 July 1921.[4]

On 26 March 1918 he was wounded yet again:

> …had a long day visiting Corps and Divisions. Hun planes were bombing Acheux heavily, and on the way back from Third Army HQ I stopped the car and had just got out to take cover in a ditch when a bomb landed 15 yards from me. I was hit in the elbow and the arm broken.

This was his third wound, and by far the most serious. The arm would be very badly set, and he was denied the proper use of it for the rest of his life. He was sent home and graded 'C.2' which meant service in the UK. As a result he was sent as an Instructor to the Staff College in Cambridge, where he remained until the end of the war.

Soon after the war ended in November 1918, Bernard went across to France on a liaison visit to GHQ, and wrote:

> Woke up full of 'joie de vivre' at being in France again… A wonderful and thrilling visit to the Ypres Salient, and felt rather a ghost, wandering through the old familiar haunts, now so desolate and empty. Most of the landmarks have gone, and it is difficult to find one's way… I feel quite certain

12

that the happiest days of my life have been those spent with the 14th (Light) Division.

On 29 January 1919 he was boarded as fit for duty at GHQ, to which he at once returned, still as a GSO 2. He visited all the headquarters, and commented after a trip to Coblenz:

My visit to Coblenz made me realize that we must be very firm with the Hun, as he has not yet learnt the enormity of his offence against civilization, and learnt his lesson. Relaxation of firmness results at once in a return to pre-war arrogance.

Notes
1. Lieutenant Colonel V.T. Bailey, who had by chance been Bernard's Company Commander at Sandhurst.
2. Throughout his life Bernard always referred to the First World War as 'the Kaiser's War', and called the Germans either 'Huns' or 'Boche'.
3. Ultimately Field Marshal Sir John Dill.
4. By a strange coincidence, I bought a house in 1969 at 4, Trevor Street, just fifty yards from where I was born.

Chapter 3

Between the Wars (1919-1939)

At the end of the First World War, Bernard (or BP as I shall now call him) was a Brevet Major, with a DSO and MC, an Italian Silver Medal for Military Valour, and had been four times Mentioned in Dispatches. He had proved himself to be a brave, dedicated and outstanding officer in the field, and had also gained much valuable experience on the staff.

In the next twenty years he would confirm his reputation as an 'Outstanding' officer, rising from Major to Major General. His career in this period centred on three Army establishments; the Military Intelligence Branch of the War Office, the Staff College at Camberley and the Imperial Defence College.

But he was essentially an infantry soldier, always happiest when serving with troops. It was not surprising however that, with his intelligence and efficiency, he found himself also cast in the role of teacher, passing on his knowledge of war to others. As part of his studies, he continued to keep a diary, partly as a record of events, but also as a memo book in which he jotted down things that appealed to him, such as people he met, conversations, newspaper articles and passages in books that were of interest.

In January 1920 he went to the Staff College at Camberley as a student, the first of three appointments he would hold there. He would return in 1936 as an Instructor, and finally, as Commandant (1938-39). He was also an Instructor at the Staff College in Quetta in India in 1933, and so it was with some justification that he complained later that he was 'more a schoolmaster than a soldier'. But it was the Army's gain, and he too acquired much valuable experience and knowledge.

From Camberley BP was sent in 1921 to the War Office as GSO 2 in MI 3, the section handling military intelligence in Western Europe. It was interesting work, involving liaison within both Germany and France, but he was glad in 1925 to return to his regiment as a Company Commander. The 1st Battalion was stationed in Cologne as part of the Army of Occupation and, although he was happy to be back at Regimental soldiering, his comment was:

> I do not like the atmosphere here, and as an Army of Occupation, we appear to be rather a farce.

On 7 July his company carried out a field firing demonstration for the officers and NCOs of the 2 Rhine Brigade, and it was described by the Colonel Commandant as 'a most instructive demonstration carried out by a very well trained company'. Significantly, BP wrote in his diary:

> The question of the training of section leaders requires very careful thought and study, as they are the mainspring of action in war.

This would become the dominant theme of all the Battle Training that he would initiate in the Second World War.

On 8 July 1925 BP was gazetted a Brevet Lieutenant Colonel in the King's Birthday Honours List in recognition of his work in MI 3. He wrote:

> No prize has given me greater pleasure, and I take an almost childish delight in my new title; professionally it is of the greatest value to me, especially as counting four years service towards Major General.

Staff College and Imperial Defence College (1926-29)

On 3 August 1925 he heard that he was to go to the Staff College again, this time as an Instructor, and he spent a valuable three years there from January 1926 to the end of 1928. This was followed by a year as a student at the Imperial Defence College in London, a course designed specially for those seen as future higher commanders in all three Services. It was of considerable interest and significance to him, in that he met and exchanged views with many of the future leaders, civil as well as military, of the next war.

Regimental Depot (1930-32)

This was followed by two very happy years commanding the Regimental Depot of the Oxfordshire and Buckinghamshire Light Infantry at Cowley near Oxford from 1930 to 1932.[1] It was a chance to renew his links with Oxford, and during his period of command, BP brought into existence, with the warm cooperation of the Dean and Chapter of Christ Church, the Regimental Chapel in the south aisle of the Cathedral, in which he, his father, his mother, and his son, Tony, are commemorated. This gave him great satisfaction, and he wrote:

> The Regimental Chapel represents to me the first ideal I have yet achieved, and I wish I could achieve more of what is beautiful and useful. In the Army I am often tempted to feel I have lost idealism of purpose since the war.

While at Oxford, BP was elected an Honorary Student of Christ Church, and also an Honorary Member of the High Table and the Senior Common Room. He much appreciated these compliments, and felt that the portrait of his father above the High Table looked down with approval.

During these years he took the major step of buying his first house. It was at 323 Woodstock Road, Oxford, acquired on 12 February 1930, and he described it as 'an interesting and also an expensive experience'. It was the only house he would ever own until his retirement in 1957, and he wrote rather wistfully in 1933, while in Quetta, 'What a great asset in life to have a family place, a lasting home from one generation to another.'

He was never well off, having virtually no private means, and he always 'found it very hard to make both ends meet'. He lived remarkably simply, and his only 'extravagance' was to spend any spare money on buying antiques, using the excuse that they were a 'good investment' (which they usually were).

Quetta (1933-34)

From 1933 to 1934 BP was an Instructor at the Senior Wing of the Staff College in Quetta, the Indian Army equivalent of Camberley.[2] He enjoyed it, and earned a reputation as an exceptionally hard worker. This was appropriate, for the family motto is *Labor Ipse Voluptas*, or 'Work Itself a Pleasure'. It was chosen by his grandfather, Sir James Paget, (1814-1899), who was renowned for his hard work, and he would seem to have passed this characteristic to most (though not all) of his descendants.

Although BP was undoubtedly a sufferer from the family motto, he did at times question its value. 'I sometimes wonder if I take my work too seriously, and devote too much time to it, or whether I organize my time badly and so waste it.' In fact, he was renowned throughout his life as an extraordinarily hard worker, and he certainly never wasted a moment of his time:

I do long sometimes for more relaxation and amusement. I have worked so hard and continuously since 1912...and I have always been too hard up to take full advantage of what opportunities I have had for recreation; it looks as if I must be content with *Labor Ipse Voluptas* for a long time to come.

The Fight to Prevent War (MI 3 1934-36)

On 15 March 1934 he was offered another appointment in the War Office, again in MI 3, but this time as GSO 1 with the rank of Lieutenant Colonel. He found himself undecided about it:

If I refuse, I shall suffer for it; if I accept, the Staff College will suffer through loss of continuity.... I wish, for my own peace of mind, that the WO would not 'pass the baby' to the individual by making an 'offer', but would issue 'orders' instead!

In the end he accepted and, on 2 July 1934, he embarked on work of far greater importance and responsibility than any he had had to face so far, for it was a matter of whether or not anything could be done to prevent the Second World War. His master, the Director of Military Operations and Intelligence, was Major General Sir John Dill, under whom Bernard had served at GHQ in France in 1917.

They shared the same high principles and religious approach to life. They also both believed strongly that there was a real possibility of another war if the right steps were not taken in Europe; and knowing full well the horror of war, they were both determined that another conflict must, if possible, be avoided at all costs.

MI3 covered the whole of Europe, the United States and also South America; it received reports from the Military Attachés in those countries, and also maintained close relations with the Foreign Attachés in London. On the basis of the knowledge and information acquired, the Branch was responsible for providing the basic material for reports to the Chiefs of Staff.

For the next two and a half years Bernard was absorbed in momentous appreciations and many internal problems, some of which could possibly lead to war. This was the period of German re-armament (1935) the Saar Plebiscite (January 1935), Italy's attack on Abyssinia (October 1935), Germany's withdrawal from the League of Nations (October 1935), the Franco-Russian Alliance of May 1935 and German conscription (March 1935).

Bernard was convinced that peace in Europe might be achieved by persuading Germany to return to the League of Nations, where differences could be argued out. This could only be done in his view by showing more understanding of Germany's grievances, and so giving her a greater sense of security and satisfaction. This view was however totally opposed to that of both the British and French Governments, who considered that the only way to prevent Germany from staging a comeback was to follow a policy of isolation and encirclement.

BP's views could perhaps, with hindsight, be described as 'appeasement', which finally failed in 1939; but in 1936 they might possibly have succeeded. They were not based on sentiment or fear, for after 1914-1918 he had no love at all for

18

'the Bosche' [*sic*]. It was essentially a commonsense, military approach to an extremely complex problem.

He advocated giving Germany a chance, but maintained that if they did not behave, then a strong line must be taken against them without delay, using military force, if necessary. He believed that it was the Allied failure to show strength at the right moment, such as the Rhineland crisis in March 1936, that led to war.

An intriguing aspect of his time in MI3 from 1934 to 1936 was his relationship with the German Military Attaché to London, whom he came to know well, both on and off duty. General Baron Leo Geyr von Schweppenburg was an officer of the 'old school' of the German Army, an aristocrat who strongly disapproved of Hitler and the Nazi movement[3]. He did not favour German military aggression, and did not support Hitler's territorial ambitions. After the war he wrote a book, entitled *The Critical Years*,[4] in which he described his time as Military Attaché, and his belief that war could have been averted.

In March 1935 Geyr reported to his masters in Berlin that the arrival in the War Office of Dill and Paget had led to a new spirit in the relationship between Britain and Germany: 'They now believed that Germany must be given a fair deal if there was to be any prospect of maintaining peace in Europe.'

Relations between MI3 and Geyr became remarkably close. In July 1935 Dill and BP attended the German Army manoeuvres in East Prussia, and they in turn arranged for him to watch training in Britain, as well as taking him to the ceremony of Trooping the Colour in 1936.

In March 1936 Geyr reported that 'the British General Staff's desire for peace was unmistakable'. But then on 7 March Germany occupied the Rhineland with no warning, and in outright defiance of the Treaty of Versailles and the Locarno Agreement. It was the third 'weekend surprise' by Germany, and it caused deep resentment in Britain, not least in MI3. BP was furious, not only that it had been allowed to happen, but also that it had, in effect, nullified all his peace efforts over the last year.

19

Geyr described his reception at the War Office soon after.[5]

I could feel a chilliness in the War Office as soon as I entered the building. Bernard Paget was bitterness personified. 'Thank you for a very pleasant Sunday', he began sarcastically. I gathered that every available person on the General Staff had been working in the War Office throughout the whole of Sunday. I asked if I might speak to Dill. 'Next week,' came the laconic reply. Colonel Paget, who had been a good friend to me both in his official capacity and in private life was now just a British officer telling me the fact that the Germans had justified the views of those who had maintained all along that Germany was a hopeless case. 'We told you so,' was what I was going to have to put up with, and so were all those who had advocated fair and equal treatment for Germany.

Geyr now reported to Berlin that 'three years work towards the establishment of good relations had been nullified'. But it is doubtful if that worried the German General Staff! Geyr now rated the chance of peace as only 50:50, and he sent a telegram to that effect to Berlin.

In October 1936 Dill left the War Office to command British Troops in Palestine, and he then retired on half pay. From Palestine he wrote to BP:

I cannot tell you how sorry I am not to have seen you before I was sent out here. But I am sorrier still that you are not here to help me through this difficult and unpleasant job. You are just the man to keep a clear head in this welter of intrigue and general inefficiency.

Bernard's reaction in his diary was:

I would sooner have that said by Dill than by any other man I know, and such testament of his confidence in me is a real incentive to be worth it.

The crisis over Germany died down, but Geyr wrote later[6] that

Dill told him:

> The British General Staff had been put in an extremely
> awkward position. They had been looking ahead and
> working intensively to bring about the German remilitariza-
> tion of the Rhineland, knowing that it was bound to come
> eventually in any case. It had been their intention to link the
> whole matter with an Air Pact for the Western Powers. But
> the Germans, by taking the law into their own hands, had
> nullified the good intentions of the British.
> When one looks back at the years that followed these
> events, one cannot help thinking that it was indeed a mis-
> fortune for the German people that the Western Powers put
> up no effective counter-action at a moment when everything
> favoured it.

Looking back after the war, with the benefit of hindsight, BP and
Dill both asked themselves whether they had been right or
wrong in their attitude to Germany while they were in MI3, and
whether they could possibly have done more to try to prevent
the Second World War. Geyr believed that their views were
right, and he wrote in 1952:[7]

> Men like Dill and his colleagues were looking far ahead into
> the future with a vision that was unclouded by emotion.
> They were convinced that another war between the British
> Empire and Germany would be a tragedy not only for the
> Empire, but for the whole of Europe. They saw quite clearly
> that such a war would only further the designs of Russia,
> and in this they showed a great deal more foresight than
> many of their compatriots who now boast that they knew all
> along what Germany was about.

BP sidelined this paragraph in ink, (rather than his usual
pencil), and wrote in the margin 'I believe this to be true'. Geyr
also claimed in his book[8] that he told Hore Belisha in 1937 that:
'If war should come again, I would maintain to my dying day
that it had been unnecessary.'
BP sidelined this sentence in ink too, and also underlined it.

He continued also to analyse the MI3 policy pre-war, and when Dill wrote to him in 1939, and asked whether he thought that it had been right, BP replied: 'I assured him that I did, and that what was happening today was accurately forecast by us as the inevitable result of the French policy of encirclement.'

In 1955 BP re-read his 1935 diaries, and wrote:

I feel I may have placed too much trust in the German good faith. I am still sure that General Fritsch (German General Staff) and von Geyr were honest.[9] But nothing can excuse our policy in relation to Italy and her aggression against Ethiopia, and our condonation of the use of mustard gas. We could have prevented that war by taking a strong line at Stresa, and in doing so, we might have prevented Hitler's war. At least, Dill and I believed so.

BP's Confidential Report when he left MI 3 described him as:

...an officer of determined personality and extremely sound judgement... he sets and demands a high standard of efficiency and attention to business. His hobby is his work, and the general international situation and the deductions there from.

A discerning and intriguing assessment of his character came also from Geyr, who wrote in his book:[10]

Bernard Paget...was the sort of soldier who might have been one of Cromwell's Ironsides...a brilliant officer, a fanatical hard worker, he was, above all, a man of enormous determination.... From his earliest days, he had absorbed the atmosphere of the unique cathedral city which was his home, and his deeply felt Christianity naturally found the Soviet outlook unsympathetic.

A remarkably perceptive and accurate portrait.

At the end of 1936 BP left MI3, and was posted to Quetta again, but this time as Commander 4 Infantry Brigade. He was delighted to get away from the War Office, and to have an independent command, but he felt that he had been 'sacked' from

MI3. He described his time in MI3 in his diary as:

>...a valuable period, though a disillusioning experience. I hope I shall be a better commander for it, if only that I am more patient and tolerant.

He arrived in Quetta in February 1937, accompanied by Winnie,[11] and they moved into 203, Hanna Road. BP enjoyed the job, particularly as he had on occasions to take over the duties of Acting Commander of Baluchistan District, which he carried out with relish. He served only a year in Quetta, and looked back on it as 'very pleasant, not least because I had no financial worries'. Then in December 1937 he was summoned home to be Commandant of the Staff College at Camberley.

Commandant, The Staff College (1938-1939)

BP took over at a decidedly difficult time, when the political and military worlds were both dominated by the threat of war, and at the same time the Armed Forces were being drastically reorganized by Hore-Belisha.

On 16 February 1938 BP was promoted from Colonel to Major General with effect from 27 December 1937, and life was good, with the comfort and prestige of Staff College House, but he had a feeling that 'such happiness is not likely to last for long'.

A major project for which BP became responsible was the setting up of a new wing of the Staff College at Minley Manor near Frimley. With his usual thoroughness he took a keen interest in every detail, not only on the academic side, but also on every other aspect from the gardens to the layout and furniture.[12] It was opened by the Duke of Gloucester, with the CIGS, General Lord Gort, on 21 January 1939.

With his considerable experience of staff work, BP took drastic steps to update and streamline the teaching at the Staff College, and eight years later the Secretary of State recorded:

>When in September 1939 I went to the Staff College, I found that General Paget had gathered round him as outstanding a

staff of Regular officers as it is possible to imagine, whose quality of intellect and character were unrivalled.

When war against Germany was declared on 3 September 1939, the Staff College was soon put onto a wartime footing, and the first course consisted entirely of Territorial Army officers. They had inevitably been selected in great haste, and by half term some forty of them had been 'purged' as 'unsuitable', whereupon BP became known as 'General Purget'!

The training of staff officers was clearly of great importance, but BP was impatient to get command of troops,[13] and he was delighted when he was appointed in November 1939 to take command of 18th Division in Norfolk.

Notes
1. This designation dated from 1908, and the creation of the 1st and 2nd Battalions, The Oxfordshire and Buckinghamshire Light Infantry, though the Battalions continued to style themselves the 43rd and the 52nd.
2. He recounted that Monty was the Chief Instructor at this time, and when giving a lecture on 'Leadership', he stated: 'A commander MUST be known to his men. And if he cannot achieve this in any other way, he should wear a funny hat' – which is just what Monty did at Alamein in 1943.
3. 'I knew that Hitler hated me. In his eyes and those of his party disciples, I was already branded as a friend of Fritsch and Beck, an aristocrat, and, worse still, a Catholic. The combination of all this in one man was too much for them.' (page 156)
4. Weidenfeld and Nicolson, 1952.
5. *The Critical Years*, page 60
6. *ibid*, pp 67-8
7. *ibid*, p 86
8. *ibid*
9. Geyr maintained that he was kept in the dark by Berlin about Germany's true, aggressive intentions. (page 127)
10. *op cit*, p 27.
11. They were seen off in London by Marshal Baron von Bieberstein and General Baron Geyr von Schweppenburg, which BP described as 'a real token of friendship'.

12. A portrait of BP by Richard Green hung in the Officers' Mess at Minley, and when I was a student at Minley in 1949 there were occasions when I would perhaps be thinking of a glass of port after dinner, but would then become aware of a steely glance from the portrait on the wall, and I would scuttle off to get down to my work on 'Army/Air Cooperation'.

13. I was at Oxford during the 'phoney war' of 1939-40, and my tutor received a letter from my father saying 'I hear that my son only has to write one essay a week! Don't you know there's a war on? Make him do at least three!' And he did too!

Chapter 4

Norway (1940)

...One of the most forlorn and ill-equipped ventures that even a British Government had ever sent out to confront an all-powerful continental military power at the outset of our wars.

(Arthur Bryant, *Illustrated London News*, 4 March 1961)

By 1940 Germany was obtaining around 600,000 tons of iron ore a year from the Gallivare region in the north of neutral Sweden. They were shipping it from the port of Narvik in Norway, which was also neutral, and the ships travelled from Narvik to Germany within Norwegian territorial waters, where they could escape the threat of interception by British naval forces.

The iron ore was vital to Germany's armament industry, and early in 1940 Britain and France decided that the shipments must be stopped. They therefore planned in March 1940 to lay minefields in three areas along the Norwegian coast, in order to close this route to German shipping.

It was appreciated that this move might well provoke a German reaction in the shape of an invasion of Norway, and to counter this, an Anglo-French force, about a division strong, was set up under Lieutenant General H.R.S. Massy. He was told to be ready to seize the Norwegian ports of Narvik, Trondheim, Bergen and Stavanger, if a request was received from the Norwegian Government to do so, as the result of a German invasion. Plans included the formation of 'Composite Companies' of volunteers from several divisions, including BP's 18th Division in Norfolk.

But the Germans had, not surprisingly, made their own appreciation of the situation, and had also concluded that Norway was vital to them, not only as a source of iron ore, but also as a base for their control of the North Sea and the Atlantic, and that it must be denied to the Allies.

On 1 March 1940 Hitler issued orders for Norway and Denmark to be invaded early in April. On 8 April the Allies, unaware of any German plans, laid their minefields along the Norwegian coast. By a strange coincidence, the Germans, unaware of any

27

Allied plans, launched their invasion of Norway the very same day.

The assault was overwhelming, carried out by ten well-equipped and fully trained divisions, and it achieved complete surprise. The unprepared Norwegian Army fought gallantly, but had little chance, and by the evening of 9th most of the ports and airfields in Norway were in German hands.

On 10 April the Norwegian Government held a Council of War at Hamar, eighty miles north of Oslo. The Army chiefs considered the position to be hopeless, and recommended surrender. But the crisis produced the 'man of the moment', Colonel Otto Ruge, who argued fiercely in favour of fighting on, provided that Norway could rely on receiving prompt and effective support from Britain and France. With the support of King Haakon, Colonel Ruge won the day, the Army chiefs resigned, and he was promoted to General and Commander-in-Chief of the Norwegian Army.

The Allies did promise to provide help, but it was easier said than done. Plans were hurriedly made for a landing at Narvik to regain that vital port. It was also hoped to seize Trondheim, because it was the narrowest part of Norway, and an Allied occupation of that area could effectively cut off the north from the south. It is the latter operation that concerns us.

The first plan was for a direct assault on Trondheim from the sea, but this was abandoned on 12 April in favour of a complicated three-pronged attack. One force, commanded by Major General A. Carton de Wiart, was to land at Namsos (seventy miles north of Trondheim), and close in from the north. At the same time, 148 Infantry Brigade, under Brigadier H. de R. Morgan, was to land at Andalsnes (120 miles south of Trondheim) with two tasks. The first was to seize the key road and rail centre at Dombas, which would prevent any German advance from the south. That done, they were to advance northwards towards Trondheim.

When these two forces had closed in on Trondheim, a seaborne assault would be launched against the port by naval and military forces under Major General F.E. Hotblack.

The first three landings were completed successfully at Narvik

(15 April), Namsos (17th) and Andalsnes (18th). But then a series of mishaps occurred. Major General Hotblack, having just been briefed at the War Office about the Trondheim operation, was found unconscious at the foot of the Duke of York's Steps, having just had a stroke. One of his brigade commanders, Brigadier H.P.M. Berney-Ficklin was briefed to replace him, but he was then seriously injured when his plane crashed at Kirkwall on the morning of the 19th.

Yet another replacement had to be found, and the choice fell this time on Major General Paget, then commanding the 18th Division in Norfolk. At 1715 hours on 19th he received a telephone call saying that he was to catch a train leaving for Scotland at 2015 that evening! He would be met on the train by a staff officer who would brief him: 'The only clue as to my task was that I should bring warm clothing with me!'

An hour later he was rung up again to say that the plans had been changed, and he was now to report to the War Office at 1030 next morning, 20 April. He did so, and learned from the CIGS that he had originally been selected to replace Major General Hotblack, and to have sailed in two days time to command the direct assault on Trondheim. Hence the first telephone call. Now he was to take command of the force that had already landed at Andalsnes and was operating in southern Norway, under the name of SICKLE FORCE. His task was 'to cooperate with the Norwegian Army in preventing the northward advance of the German army based in southern Norway', and he was to be ready to move in two and a half days time.

He then spent what he described as 'the most hectic two and a half days of my life', (though they would in fact be followed by an even more hectic seven days in Norway!) For a start, he had to form his non-existent Divisional Headquarters from scratch, collect together his staff and make a plan. There was virtually no intelligence information available, and his excellent Chief of Staff, Lieutenant Colonel C.G.C. Nicholson, wrote:

Everything was in a state of improvisation. There were no maps; we had to tear them out of geography books and send the ADC to the Norwegian Travel Agency to buy a Baedeker and collect any brochures he could find.[1]

BP's command was supposed to consist of a complete division with three infantry brigades and the normal supporting elements, such as artillery, transport, signals and medical services. But one complete brigade failed to materialize, as did most of the supporting arms. Then a vital supply ship, SS *Cedarbank*, carrying guns, ammunition and rations, was sunk in the North Sea. In the event, SICKLE FORCE landed with no artillery at all, no tanks or armoured cars, no transport, no medical services, no proper signals equipment and only four anti-aircraft guns.

The actual Order of Battle of SICKLE FORCE in Norway was:

> Divisional Headquarters. (Major General B.C.T. Paget).
> 15 Infantry Brigade (Regular) (Brigadier H.E.F. Smyth)
> > 1st Bn, The King's Own Yorkshire Light Infantry
> > 1st Bn, The Yorkshire and Lancashire Regiment
> > 1st Bn, The Green Howards
> 148 Infantry Brigade (TA) (less one battalion) (Brigadier H. de R. Morgan)
> > 1st Bn, The Leicestershire Regiment
> > 1st Bn, The Sherwood Foresters
> 168th Light Anti Aircraft Battery (less two troops) i.e. four guns
> 55th Field Company, Royal Engineers (less one section)

23-25 April

BP set off by train for Rosyth on 23 April, his departure being delayed for ten minutes to enable a staff officer to bring him the discouraging news that the Germans had already advanced forty miles further north from Oslo than expected.

He sailed on 24th in HMS *Manchester*, together with 15 Brigade,[2] and arrived at 2000 hours on 25th at Molde, where he transferred to a Norwegian gunboat to reach Andalsnes.[3] He was met by Brigadier Morgan, commanding 148 Brigade,[4] and some of his staff, including Colonel Beichman, a Norwegian

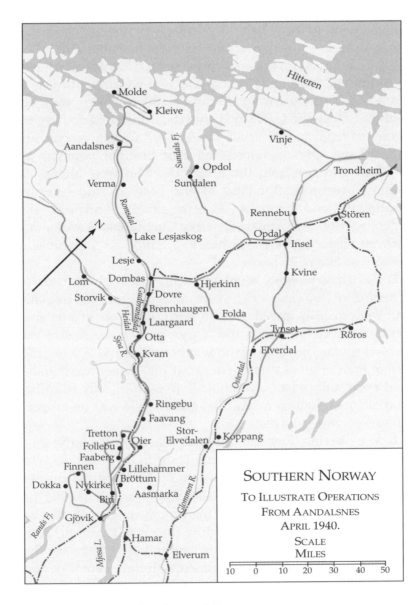

Liaison Officer, sent by General Ruge.

At 2230 on 25th BP received from them his first on-the-spot briefing, and it was not encouraging. Brigadier Morgan reported that his brigade, about 1,000 strong, had landed at Andalsnes on 18th, and had immediately been placed under command of 2nd Norwegian Division, and sent south to

31

Lillehammer to try to halt the relentless German advance north from Oslo. But from the start they were heavily outnumbered by the enemy, consisting of a corps, some 8,500 strong, who had medium and light tanks and artillery, of which the British had none. The Germans were able to fire their artillery over open sights at ranges of 2,000 yards, and the British had nothing with which to retaliate. Above all, the enemy had complete air superiority, and any movement by day brought bombing and machine-gun fire from the Luftwaffe, who were almost constantly overhead. Bombing of the base at Andalsnes was continuous, and the town was being rapidly destroyed. 'What might we not have achieved,' wrote Christopher Buckley in the Official History, 'if we had had just a little air support and a battery or two of 25-pounders?'

It was a discouraging situation for 148 Brigade, who had, from 19th to 23rd, fought a series of actions with great determination, but were steadily forced back. By 23rd they were in a defensive position at Tretton, with the Norwegians some twelve miles behind them. They had by now suffered around 700 casualties out of their original strength of about 1,000; their two battalions had been reduced to a combined strength of only six officers and 300 men, which meant that the brigade was no longer an effective fighting force as such.

Before leaving England BP had asked particularly for air support and had been promised sixty fighter aircraft. Efforts were made to provide them, starting with the dispatch on the evening of 24th of eighteen Gladiators,[5] which landed on a frozen lake near Leskasjog. But the very next morning they were attacked by German aircraft before they could take-off, and all but three were destroyed on the ground. The three survivors flew forty-nine sorties, and six enemy aircraft were shot down, but the Germans retained their complete air superiority, and no further aircraft arrived to support SICKLE FORCE.

Meanwhile, 15 Brigade, under Brigadier Smyth, having disembarked at Andalsnes on 25th, moved up to Kvam, where 1 KOYLI under Major E.E.E. Cox took up defensive positions, with the rest of the brigade behind them. That night 1 KOYLI came under attack, but they held their positions without difficulty.

32

Liaison with the Norwegians

Having landed in Norway, BP's first move was to set off for the front, accompanied by Brigadier Morgan and his own Chief of Staff, Colonel Nicholson, to meet General Ruge, the newly-appointed C.-in-C. of the Norwegian Army. On the way, he called in on the British Minister, Sir Cecil Dormer, in the Park Hotel in Andalsnes. The Minister emphasized that General Ruge was the key figure in the Norwegian resistance to the Germans; he considered that he was a strong man, who would fight to the last, but who urgently needed and expected British support. If it did not come, and come soon, the Norwegian will and ability to continue the struggle might well, in his opinion, crumble.

Leaving Sir Cecil, BP and his party moved forward to General Ruge's headquarters in a small farmhouse some ten miles south of Dovre. The first meeting between the two commanders took place at 0500 on 26th and it was a crucial one. Ruge began by complaining bitterly at the smallness of the British forces, and was angry that he had not been kept informed of their plans. He said that his troops had borne the brunt of the fighting so far, and could not carry on until they had been rested, reorganized and re-equipped.

BP listened, and then went on to visit 2nd Norwegian Division, which had been withdrawn into reserve, and he received the same story from them:

> I felt that I could only agree with these views, and concluded that I could expect little support from Norwegian troops. I did however obtain a promise from General Ruge that Norwegian ski troops would protect my flanks, operating under my command. All other Norwegian troops south of Dombas were then withdrawn, and I was given entire responsibility for the Gudbrandsdal valley.

He went next to Headquarters 15 Brigade at Kvam, and found Lieutenant Colonel A.I. Kent-Lemon in command, as Brigadier Smyth had been wounded. The troops were in excellent heart, and he felt that Kvam was safe in the hands of the KOYLI. He set up his own headquarters at Dovre, so as to be near General Ruge, and one of his staff wrote:

It is difficult to over-estimate the tremendous personal effect that General Paget's personality had on the operations in the Gudbrandsdal Valley... It was clear to everyone that the commander had arrived, and was fighting the battle according to his own plans.

26 April

BP felt that he was now in a position to make an appreciation of the situation, and his conclusions were:

My object at this stage was still to stop the enemy. I judged that I could not expect my forward troops to withstand the enemy for more than 48 hours in any one position without any form of artillery and air support, yet opposed by an enemy well equipped with both. My planning was therefore directed to delaying the enemy as much as possible, so as to give time for the arrival of my artillery and air support. Thus equipped, I anticipated little difficulty in stopping the enemy.

On 26th he therefore sent an urgent signal to the War Office stressing the need for them to send out the third brigade of his division without delay, together with some artillery and above all, fighter aircraft and anti-aircraft guns. But he would not see any of them.

Meanwhile, with 148 Brigade out of action, BP now had some 3,000 men with which to oppose the enemy's 8,500 motorized troops, and he realized that his ability to delay the enemy any longer depended on the arrival of support. His confidence was boosted by a magnificent defensive action by 1 KOYLI, in which they knocked out five German tanks and three armoured cars, before withdrawing in good order.

The pressure at the front might have been reduced slightly by this action, but the situation elsewhere was grim, due largely to the vulnerability of his lines of communication with his base at Andalsnes.

After the campaign, BP emphasized this point in a talk to the Staff College at Minley in June 1940:

It would be difficult to imagine any Lines of Communication more exposed to air attack, to which it was subjected continually during the hours of daylight by heavy bombing and machine-gun attacks, and we had no anti-aircraft available for protecting it. Nor did we have the means of repairing the damage done to road and railway, other than the limited resources of the Norwegians. The base at Andalsnes and the key point of Dombas were completely destroyed, and Otta very nearly so... I had no troops available to protect this long L. of C. (100 miles) and was always anxious lest the enemy might get behind me with ski troops or parachutists and cut me off from the base. I do not know why they did not do so.

This was but one of the problems. There was not enough transport, and most of it had to be provided by the Norwegians; communications were limited and unreliable, and use had to be made of the civilian telephone system, though this was inevitably far from secure; there was only one Field Ambulance forward of the base area, and the British force had to rely to a large extent on the Norwegian Red Cross for medical cover.

It was a scenario that even the most sadistic of instructors at the Staff College would not have dared to devise for his students, but in this case, it was 'for real'!

27 April

So serious was the destruction at Andaalsnes that the Garrison Commander there reported to BP on the evening of 26th that, unless the air situation could be put right, the base would soon be unworkable. The next morning, the 27th, he could not contact BP at all, and so sent a signal on his own initiative to the War Office, the Admiralty and the Air Ministry, recommending an evacuation.

As it happened, General Massy at the War Office was coming to the same conclusion:

Without air cover, I had little doubt that any further operations would become impossible and that we should be compelled to evacuate our forces from Central and Southern Norway.

During the morning of 27th BP received a report that the enemy were advancing on Folda from Elverdal on his left flank, and he promptly went by car on a personal reconnaissance. But he could not get through due to deep snow. 'I felt acutely the need for air reconnaissance to find out what was going on, on the other side of the hill.' All he could do was to send Brigadier Morgan with 400 men to defend Dombas.

The 1st Yorks and Lancs withdrew during the night of 27th/28th, but came under fierce pressure from the Germans, who cut off some of the forward troops, so that only 12 officers and 300 men got back to Otta that night. More returned during the next twenty-four hours, but the battalion was no longer effective, and all now depended on The Green Howards.

28 April

Early on the 28th a radio message came from the War Office that the evacuation of SICKLE FORCE had been decided on 'in principle', and that there were three alternatives. First, that enough shipping would be available to move the whole force in one night. Second, that it would take place over two or three nights, and third, that more troops would be landed, with anti-aircraft guns, to enable SICKLE FORCE to hold on. It was also pointed out that a definite decision to evacuate might have to be taken before any reply from BP could reach the War Office, and that he must therefore be ready to leave at short notice.

The gist of the message was delivered to BP verbally by an officer who had come up from the base, and he was carrying the actual message in his boot for safety. He could not however extract it before BP had to move off.

I left him to get his boot off and retrieve the message, and told him to follow me up the road with it. But he missed his way, and nearly ended up in the front line.

Shortly afterwards, came another message saying that the definite decision had been taken in London to evacuate, and that the first plan would be adopted. But BP was told not to inform General Ruge at this stage.

He replied to both messages by pointing out that evacuation would only be possible with the full cooperation of General Ruge, and that, if the evacuation decision was final, he must first, as promised to Ruge, cover the evacuation of some 4,000 Norwegian troops to neighbouring islands.

Time was now extremely short, and BP decided that the only feasible and honourable course was to go and see General Ruge immediately, and explain the situation:

It was evident that I could only hope to carry out the evacuation with the cooperation of General Ruge, on whom I depended for transport by road and rail and for flank protection… I decided that the right course to take was to be perfectly frank… I therefore went to his headquarters, and acted accordingly.

I went in considerable anxiety as to what his reaction would be; it was quite on the cards that he would refuse to play, as he already felt very sore about our not having sent more troops to assist him, and if he did so, there was little hope for SICKLE FORCE, as we were entirely dependent on the Norwegians for road and rail transport, as well as for communications and medical services.

I told him quite frankly what the situation was, and that in all probability, I would shortly receive definite orders to evacuate my force; but that in any case I guaranteed to cover the withdrawal of the Norwegian forces on my front, and would hold Dombas until this was done.

After an initial outburst in which he spoke of being betrayed, and declared that an Allied evacuation would totally destroy the morale of the Norwegian Army and people, he regained his composure, and promised to give what support he could.

Overall, he took it extremely well, and I can never be sufficiently appreciative of his loyalty and cooperation, not only on this occasion, but all through the operation. As I left his Headquarters, his Chief of Staff, a very formal officer, said to my Chief of Staff, 'I still shake you by the hand', and then he did so.

Meanwhile, pressure was building up at Otta. But The Green Howards, despite being now extremely thin on the ground, fought a fine rearguard action, destroying one medium and two light tanks with their 25mm anti-tank weapons.

A key factor in the withdrawal was the demolition of the bridges over the Rosta Gorge between Dovre and Otta, which should delay the enemy for forty-eight hours. At 1800 hours, 1 KOYLI were ordered forward to cover the withdrawal, which was successfully completed that night, together with the blowing of the bridges by 55 Field Company RE.

29 April

The next day BP received a blunt reply from the War Office to his urgent request of the day before for air cover and artillery support. It read:

> Fighter support impossible. Essential you realize this and make best getaway possible. Massy.

During the night of 28th/29th the Norwegian ski troops providing flank protection were withdrawn, and so were many of the Norwegian troops protecting the L. of C.

On the 29th an officer arrived from the War Office with the withdrawal plans, which were now changed to extend over three nights, and BP and Ruge had to adjust their plans accordingly. Then Ruge found that he could not get all his troops away until twenty-four hours later than planned, which meant that the British would have to hold on to Dombas for a further twenty-four hours. BP undertook to do this, and Ruge 'lent' him four Norwegian mountain guns, which were gratefully received as his only artillery.

BP had another meeting with Ruge that afternoon, and found him personally friendly, but angry that he had not been told about the British evacuation plans. He said that the Norwegians would give up unless the British went on fighting. The evacuation started that night, but due to fierce enemy air attacks, only a few hundred got away; they included the King of Norway and the British and French Legations.

30 April

At 0600 hours BP held a conference at Headquarters 15 Brigade to plan the withdrawal from DOMBAS that evening at 2130 hours. All went well, including the demolition of key bridges, using naval depth charges as the only explosives available. The four Norwegian guns did sterling work, and their unexpected appearance did much to keep the Germans at bay.

An enemy reconnaissance aircraft was shot down by rifle fire, which fortunately discouraged further air attacks for a while.

1 May

But then came trouble. The train left at 2300 hours, but was derailed by a bomb crater at Leskasjog. So, at 0100 hours, the weary troops had to get out and march seventeen miles to the tunnel at Verma, the only possible hiding place during the day. BP wrote:

> I have never seen men more exhausted; yet in spite of this, they never lost heart, and they brought all their equipment back with them. We owed a lot to railway tunnels, first at Dombas and then at Verma. In the latter was a loaded ammunition train, and also the train on which we relied to get us to Andalsnes; and by the time we had got 1,700 troops in as well, we were packed like sardines, and it was scarcely possible to move without walking on prostrate men who were so tired that they slept on the rough metalling.

Throughout the day there was a long anxious wait, with protection dependent on a rearguard of Royal Marines brought up from Andalsnes. The train was due to leave at 2230, but BP brought the time forward to 2030, despite the risk of being seen while it was still light. Then:

When the driver began to get up steam at 1730, the tunnel filled with impenetrable smoke. We were driven out, willy-nilly, into the open, where we expected to find the German bombers waiting for us. Fortunately, they were not overhead just then, and the men dispersed steadily and quickly.

At about 1800 there was another alarm when the rearguard came under such pressure from the Germans that they had to be reinforced by the Green Howards and the Yorks and Lancs. They managed to keep the enemy at bay until the longed for darkness came, when the train prepared to leave – with the driver under an armed guard just to ensure that he kept going.

To general relief, the train reached Andalsnes without further incident.

2 May

Andalsnes itself was in complete ruins, but there was just one small jetty left from which it was possible to embark the troops. All went well, with destroyers ferrying the exhausted men out to the bigger ships lying out in the fjord, and the operation was completed before dawn with no casualties.

BP wrote later:

> That it was possible to withdraw my force in the face of a superior enemy over a distance of 100 miles, to fight five rearguard actions, and to get away with it, was due primarily to the fine leadership and initiative of subordinate commanders…and, as always in a tight place, our salvation lay in the splendid and dauntless spirit of the British soldier, for whom we, as commanders and staff officers, can never do too much.

The last troops embarked at 0200 on 2 May, making a total of 5,084 evacuated over the three days; casualties during the whole campaign in southern Norway totalled 101 killed and 1,301 wounded or missing.[6] BP himself boarded the cruiser HMS *Manchester* again, and was taken at 27 knots to Scapa Flow, from where he headed to London to report to the War Office.

Aftermath

On the afternoon of 2 May, the Prime Minister, Neville Chamberlain, made a statement in the House of Commons, in which he said:

> Thanks to the powerful forces which the Navy was able to bring to bear, and the determination and skilful dispositions of General Paget, in command of the British Forces in the area, backed by the splendid courage and tenacity of the troops, we have now withdrawn the whole of our forces from Andalsnes, under the very noses of the German aeroplanes, without, as far as I am aware, losing a single man in this operation.

The next day BP featured in most of the national papers, and was variously described as 'the unknown general' (*Daily Express*), 'a man of infinite courage,...warm-hearted, genuinely humorous, and blue-eyed...' (*Sunday Times*), 'a man of few words, who means every one of them' (*Daily Mail*), and 'a hero of two wars' (*Daily Mirror*).

The Observer thought that the operation should be known as 'Paget's Withdrawal', while a letter in *The Times* from C.T. Chevallier compared the Andalsnes operation with Sir John Moore's Retreat to Corunna in 1809. The writer made the point that both commanders were Light Infantrymen, but that happily BP had not been 'buried sadly at dead of night', and would hopefully lead the Army to final victory, as had The Duke of Wellington.

BP duly wrote his official report on the campaign, which was incorporated into the official report published as a Supplement to the *London Gazette* of 28 May 1946. He also gave a talk, somewhat reluctantly, to the Staff College at Minley in June 1940, and in both he listed the three main lessons that he considered must be learnt.

First he emphasized the need for a sound appreciation from those ordering any operation which should cover the information needed to make not only a battle plan (without having to buy a Baedeker!), but also an administrative plan.

Second, he stressed the vital influence of air forces in close support of the ground troops on land operations, (not yet fully appreciated), and the difficulties of operating in the face of total enemy air superiority:

I have no hesitation in saying that a degree of cooperation between the Army and the Air Force, comparable to that which is now the case with Germany, is essential, if we are not to remain at a dangerous disadvantage.

His warning would be confirmed all too clearly by the German blitzkrieg against the BEF only a month later.

Finally, he pointed out the dangers of 'improvisation' and the 'ad hoc' sort of force he had had under command in Norway.

We are apt to pride ourselves on our ability to improvise in an emergency, but we might often avoid the necessity for doing so, if we showed more fore-thought in appreciating the situation.

As a constructive comment, he proposed the planning of a reserve force, available for use in emergencies, such as Norway, and that this should include detailed administrative resources, and reconnaissance capabilities; this is standard practice today, but it was a lesson still to be learned in 1940.

After the war, BP was determined to try to obtain a British honour for General Ruge and several other Norwegian officers who had supported him in the campaign. It took a lot of doing, but the General was finally awarded a KCB.

On 28 February 1948 BP wrote to General Ruge:

Had it not been for your loyal comradeship and cooperation in the dark days of our retreat from Norway, we could not have successfully evacuated the British troops from Andalsnes...you played the game by me throughout, and did all that I asked by way of assistance in flank protection, provision of transport and evacuation of my wounded, and for this I cannot adequately express my appreciation and gratitude.

When Ruge finally received his honour, he wrote to BP:

My dear General,

I beg you to accept my best thanks for your kind letter and for your friendly congratulations on the occasion of my nomination for this high British decoration... I have often said to my countrymen that, in those days when you and I were fighting for what could seem to be a lost cause, I learnt to know you as the best and most loyal of comrades in arms. I feel I have a right to repeat those words when I am writing to you today.
   Yours sincerely
   Otto Ruge

Many years later, BP also received a letter from Colonel Nicholson, who had been his Chief of Staff during the campaign (who was now General Sir Cameron Nicholson):

Never shall I forget how you tackled Ruge in the really vital moments of the campaign. Those of us who were with you at that crucial time have never ceased to realize that but for your firm control of the situation, we would all most certainly have spent the rest of the war in a cage! This is not an over-statement. (Letter to BP 31.12.59)

Notes
1. It is almost unbelievable, but the German C.-in-C. Norway, General von Falkenhorst, recorded that he did exactly the same! 'I went to town and bought a Baedeker, a tourist guide, in order to find out what Norway was like...I had no idea...I absolutely did not know what to expect.' (*Norway 1940*, François Kersardy, page 33)
2. The Regular Brigade sent from the BEF in France.
3. Andalsnes was defended by some 700 Royal Marines.
4. The Territorial Army Brigade sent from the UK.
5. From 263 Fighter Squadron, RAF.
6. The Germans triumphantly described it as 'an unresting pursuit of the wildly retreating British'.

Chapter 5

Home Forces (1940-1943)

We are about to engage in the most decisive battle in the Empire's existence, with hopelessly inadequate means…

(BP 1.6.40)

BP's involvement with Home Forces fell into four phases:

I.	27.5.40	Chief of Staff to Field Marshal Ironside
II.	20.7.40	Chief of Staff to General Brooke
III.	20.1.41	GOC South Eastern Command
IV.	24.11.41	C.-in-C. Home Forces until 23.7.43

Phase One. Chief of Staff to Field Marshal Ironside (27.5.40 to 20.7.40)

On 18 May 1940, after two weeks leave, BP resumed command of the 18th Division in Norfolk. But it was to be for nine days only, for on 27th he was appointed Chief of Staff to Field Marshal Sir Edmund Ironside, who on the same day became C.-in-C. Home Forces in place of General Sir Walter Kirke.

It was a desperate moment in Britain's history. On 10 May the Germans had launched their blitzkrieg against Belgium and France, and by the end of the month, the British and French armies were being evacuated from the beaches of Dunkirk. Headquarters Home Forces and the War Office were faced with the mammoth task of reorganizing and re-equipping some

350,000 men, and at the same time preparing for the defence of the country against a German invasion that seemed both inevitable and imminent. It was the greatest threat ??to our survival at any time in history.[1]

Vast quantities of equipment and transport had been lost, as well as tanks and artillery, and the Army was barely operational until the losses had been made good. Nor was it a matter only of the defence of the UK, for the war had still to be fought overseas, primarily in the Middle East, and reinforcements had to be provided from the UK for formations worldwide.

When the dust had died down, a list was compiled by Home Forces of what had been achieved during this crisis, and the basic statistics give a fair idea of the scale of the task:

a. 1,522 units evacuated from France were sorted out and reorganized.

b. 873 of these 1,522 units had to be re-equipped.

c. 396 units were mobilized for the defence of the UK.

d. 60 units were mobilized to be sent to the Middle East.

e. Two complete divisions, totalling some 40,000 men, were re-equipped within seven days, and sent back to France to continue the struggle.

f. One Divisional HQ, one infantry brigade and several units were sent to Iceland.

g. One complete division was sent to Ireland.

h. Altogether, 252 guns, 255 tanks and nearly 15,000 vehicles were issued.

In addition to the needs of the Regular Army, the Home Guard was enormously expanded, its equipment improved, and its organization overhauled in anticipation of invasion. GHQ Home Forces itself had to be reorganized and expanded, and two new Corps HQ were set up. Territorial Army units were mobilized and given their roles, while plans for the defence of the island were revised and put into effect.

The brunt of the work involved fell onto the War Office and GHQ Home Forces, and BP was far from happy with what he found in both organizations:

Apart from the fact that we are about to engage in the most decisive battle of the Empire's existence with hopelessly inadequate means, I find that GHQ Home Forces is equally hopeless in its organization and preparedness, e.g. only one trained clerk on the G side, no proper establishment, etc.... To bed at 2 a.m.' (Diary 1.6.40)

Went to the War Office and 'strafed', as I do daily, about the lack of appreciation of the time factor and the needs of GHQ.' (Diary 5.6.40)

'I 'strafed' over the delay in getting things done; it all moves too slowly. What a rare quality is common sense!' (Diary 4.6.40)

The tragic and astounding apathy of the Government and people continues in the face of the growing threat of the collapse of France. No one in the War Office seems to have any clear grasp of the realities of the situation, and work goes on as usual, with decisions being clogged by endless committees and officers going out to lunch. (Diary 6.6.40)

On 20 June he was appointed a CBE.

Phase II. Chief of Staff to General Brooke (20.7.40 to 21.1.41)

On 20 July 1940 Field Marshal Ironside was replaced as C.-in-C. Home Forces by General Sir Alan Brooke, who had just returned from commanding 1st Corps in the BEF. He wrote:

When I arrived, Ironside had already gone, but Paget was thoroughly familiar with all dispositions, and able to put me in the picture. I would not have wished for a more helpful and loyal COS, and am deeply grateful to him for the efficient way in which he ran the HQ.

They were both highly professional and experienced soldiers, and they worked together well as a team, with mutual understanding and respect. On 13 August the Battle of Britain began, and seemed obviously intended as the prelude to invasion. On 7 September the Chiefs of Staff decided that an assault was now such a real possibility that they ordered GHQ Home Forces to send out the dire codeword CROMWELL, which meant 'Invasion imminent and probable within 12 hours.'[2]

All troops were already at eight hours notice, and 'stood to' at dawn and dusk, but now Southern and Eastern Commands were put on 'Immediate' alert. The air raids on London began the next day, and the country braced itself for the final challenge. Brooke wrote in his diary:

> The responsibility of feeling what any mistakes, or even mis-appreciations, may mean to the future of these isles and of the Empire, is a colossal one, and staggers me at times.

Much the same feelings must have applied to BP as his Chief of Staff!

The invasion never came, and by October the threat had virtually disappeared. But it was not until the winter of 1941 that it was considered safe to start withdrawing troops from their defensive commitments and start training them for offensive action.

GHQ Home Forces was in St Paul's School, Hammersmith, and both Brooke and BP lived and fed there. The days were filled with endless interviews and conferences on a vast range of subjects, from the tasks to be given to the Home Guard to the possible use of gas by the Germans and also their potential to carry out airborne operations; there were measures to be taken against bombing and landings as well as research into new weapons and new techniques. Re-equipment continued, alongside such questions as the policy for restricted areas and plans for the evacuation of civilians. At the same time, the main activity was training, ceaseless and tough and in all weathers, with the aim of creating an effective new army by the spring of 1941. This meant many more training areas were needed, and some five million acres were acquired to provide realistic field firing.

Phase III. GOC South Eastern Command (20.1.41 to 24.11.43)

In view of the particular vulnerability of the coasts of Kent and Sussex to invasion, and the obvious threat to London, it was decided early in 1941 to divide Eastern Command into two, and to create a new command called South Eastern, consisting of Kent and Sussex, with its headquarters at Reigate. BP was selected to command it, and he duly took over on 27 January 1941.

Brooke wrote 'He will be a great loss at GHQ', and BP recorded that when he went to say goodbye to him:

> The Chief had tears in his eyes and said he could not thank me enough for the work I had done at GHQ. I was surprised at his feelings, because I thought he had got tired of me. But evidently his staccato manner conceals a very warm heart. (Diary 18.2.41)

It could be said that the same applied to both men.

On 21 February 1941 BP wrote typically in his diary of matters large and small:

> The subjects to be tackled are legion, but it will be much easier when I know something of them. I wish that the Army was smarter in such matters as turn-out and saluting. We do not seem to make much progress in these things. Walked up the hill behind our house before dinner – a lovely, peaceful spot in which to contemplate the follies of mankind.

On 10 May the entry was:

> Went to London and bought a new rod from Hardy; a dreadful extravagance, but I want one to carry with me for the chance of a few hours fishing.

Training was now a top priority, and BP soon made clear his views on the new approach required. After one exercise his comment was:

> I spoke at the end on the need for realism and operational

48

discipline in our training, and of the importance of an appreciation of the ground.

His thoughts were already very much directed towards the concept of Battle Drill, which would become one of his 'crusades', and one of his major contributions to final victory.

His Training Directive No. 4 of 1941 dealt particularly with another of his dominant themes, the vital need for Army/Air cooperation:

> The German soldier is not a better fighting man than the British soldier, but...he is better trained in battle techniques. It is vital to appreciate the importance of cooperation with other arms, and to find frequent opportunities for practice. To this principle is attributable the remarkable coordination of the German military machine in action... .We must be ready to take the initiative if we get the chance...a special study is to be made of the French coast opposite South Eastern Command and of the enemy holding it.

The coast of South Eastern Command was the nearest point in Britain to the enemy in Occupied France, and it was possible on a clear day to see the French coastline. As a result, there was a stream of VIP visitors to Dover, and BP had to look after them.

On 4 October 1941 came a call to go and see the PM at Chequers to discuss a scheme that Churchill had thought up of launching an attack on Trondheim in Norway, in order to relieve the pressure on the Russians. The proposal was that BP should be the commander.

> He could not have chosen anyone better qualified to crab it than I am!...PM in very good form, in blue jumper suit...after dinner he gave me the whole background of his plan for invading Norway and capturing Trondheim; he was very reasonable and said that, if after careful study, I came to the conclusion that it was not militarily practicable, he would be quite agreeable to call it off. He was very complimentary of my previous effort in Norway and said that Brooke and I were the only two British soldiers who had really stood up to the German Army in this war. I felt that he

exaggerated as far as I was concerned. He was also emphatically opposed to any tampering with the morale and discipline of the Army... . Said goodnight at 1.45am. (Diary 4.10.41)

BP then attended three meetings with the Chiefs of Staff to discuss the project, which was given the codeword AJAX. An appreciation was produced and it 'unanimously rejected the project as being impracticable'. But BP noted:

Everyone except the Chief is afraid of adopting a 'non possumus' attitude vis-à-vis the PM. Tomorrow's meeting promises to be very interesting !!

It certainly was!

PM went through the "AJAX" Appreciation (by the Chiefs of Staff) and emphasized how it brought out all the difficulties and produced no detailed plan which he had asked for. He gave the Chief some fast bowling, which was well played.

Brooke remained insistent that the operation was impracticable and, at one point, Churchill looked angrily at Brooke and BP, and growled 'I sometimes think that some of my generals don't want to fight the Germans'.

Brooke described the meeting in his diary:

A very unpleasant grilling to stand up to in a full room, but excellent training for what I had to stand up to on many occasions in later years.

But to general relief AJAX was dropped.

One week later BP was told by the CIGS (now General Sir John Dill) that he had been selected as C.-in-C. Far East in place of Air Chief Marshal Sir Robert Brooke-Popham. Dill said that he had had some difficulty in getting him nominated, to which BP replied:

I dare say the PM was not in favour of me after the Trondheim affair.

His personal reaction was:

I am interested to note that this high appointment gives me no qualms.

He spent a night at Chequers discussing the Far East with Churchill, but a week later he was told that he would not be going after all, but was to succeed Brooke as C.-in-C. Home Forces. General Dill was retiring, and would be replaced as CIGS by Brooke. It was a happy arrangement all round, as it meant that BP would continue to work under Brooke, for whom he had a great respect, and he would himself take over a job with which he was already well acquainted.

BP heard that he was also in the running at one moment for CIGS, but that the PM did not approve, saying: 'He would always be quarrelling with me.[3] To which BP retorted: 'So I may well be as C.-in-C. Home Forces.'

Phase IV. C.-in-C. Home Forces (24.11.41 to 23.7.43)

On 27 November 1941 BP handed over South Eastern Command to his good friend, Major General Sir Bernard Montgomery, (as he would do again with 21st Army Group in December 1943!). He himself moved back into GHQ Home Forces in Storey's Gate, but this time with the grave responsibility of being C.-in-C. rather than Chief of Staff.

On 3 January 1942 he received a personal, and very generous letter from Monty:

My dear Bernard,

I know you will have a very great number of letters, but I feel I cannot let this occasion pass without writing to you.

I am delighted at all that has come to you recently. I look to Brookie and yourself to see us through this party, and I have complete confidence that you will both do so.

I have a very great and real affection and admiration for you personally. And so long as there is breath left in my body, you can rely on me to help you 100%.

You have only to command, and I shall be at your side.

Yours ever

Monty

Eight months later, in August 1942, Monty left the UK to take over the Eighth Army in North Africa, and he wrote again to BP to say how much he had enjoyed working under him, but that he was delighted to be going off to a theatre of war and an active front.

It will be great fun crossing swords with Rommel...

BP's comments in his diary was:

Monty is a fine soldier, and I shall miss him very much. (Diary 29.8.42)

BP wrote soon after hearing about his new job:

I should have preferred the more independent command in the Far East.

But when Japan entered the war on 7 December 1941, he changed his mind:

I am rather relieved that I did not go to the Far East, as I would have landed into the crisis of war with Japan without having had time to look around.

When his promotion to C.-in-C. was announced, BP had quite a fan mail and a good press, one Sunday paper declaring 'Paget's Our Man'. But his own first comments about his new job were less enthusiastic:

Had my first day as C.-in-C. Home Forces, and did not enjoy it. The War Office and Chiefs of Staff are difficult bodies to cope with...I should have started tonight for Singapore. (24.11.40)

We in GHQ are involved in far too many committees, and too much paper. It seems that nothing can be done unless a committee discusses it. Also too much of what is my job seems to be dealt with by the Chiefs of Staff or the War Office...I find rather a sense of lethargy and lack of direction after Army HQ.

Drove behind the Union Jack and 'Priority' light, and felt somewhat important. (26.11.41)

Today I inspected a new uniform for airborne troops, and approved a plum-coloured beret. (4.12.41)

On Christmas Day 1941 BP received the acting rank of Full General, and he wrote:

The last lap. But it has never been one of my ambitions.

In the New Year's Honours List he became a KCB.

From Brooke he inherited the C.-in-C.'s special train 'Rapier', which was 'the height of luxury and beautifully fitted up'. It had a bedroom and sitting room, as well as an ante-room/dining room and a covered wagon for two cars; there was also accommodation for his staff, who included clerks, and this added considerably to his capacity for getting his work done, while travelling some 80,000 miles a year round Britain.

He also had a Rolls Royce which had been provided for the C.-in-C. by Sir Michael Bowater, and which he regarded as the ultimate luxury; in due course he handed it over to Montgomery, together with his stalwart and much-appreciated driver, Sergeant Parker.

On 24 January 1941 he was visited by Sir Gerald Wollaston, Garter King of Arms, and between them they designed a new sign for GHQ Home Forces, consisting of a Scottish roundel with a winged lion on a blue and red background:

We thus combine England, Scotland and Wales: I like it very much, and have decided to adopt it in place of the present harp of Kneller Hall. (24.2.42)

By now it was decided that the threat of invasion had declined sufficiently for the start of training for offensive operations on a larger scale, and a series of exercises were run, designed to test everyone from junior leaders up to higher formation commanders. Battle Drill was now a major factor in all lower level training. This is covered more fully in Chapter 7.

The pressure was considerable, and BP's Chief of Staff complained that 'he had never worked so hard in his life as he had since Paget took over'.

BP took very little time off himself, but in April 1942 he accepted a day's salmon fishing on the Torridge in Devon. He had just started in on the best pool on the beat, when a dispatch rider rode up with an 'Immediate' message. It was from The King's Private Secretary and read:

His Majesty has not had an opportunity of seeing you for some time, and would be glad if you could call here at 11am on 22 April (the next day).

It was an order that BP had no hesitation in obeying, but he did follow the example of Sir Francis Drake, and finished fishing down the pool. Happily, he caught a 9 lb salmon, and set off contentedly for Buckingham Palace!

In April 1942, the Prime Minister wanted to scrap the Churchill tank, and BP was ordered to accompany him to a trial which was to decide their fate. On the way there Churchill was very scathing about their performance, and was determined to do away with them. BP pleaded for their retention, promising modifications to improve their reliability, and pointing out that he had nothing else if they went.

But the PM would not hear of it. Very fortunately only one broke down (out of 30) over a 3-mile course. A miracle in those days! On the way back to London, the PM, fortified by a large whisky and soda, agreed that they should be retained in the service, and should continue to bear his name, provided that the necessary modifications were made. (Speech to 6 Guards Tank Brigade, who manned Churchill tanks.)

On 3 February 1942 BP noted:

Had letter from CIGS in which he called me Bernard for the first time, and I replied to him as Alan. I much appreciated this token.

BP was totally uncompromising over matters on which he held strong views, and this did not always help his relationship with his superiors.

Wrote a strong letter to AG [Adjutant General] about his exuberance of paper, interference in my command and nagging of CO's [Commanding Officers]; sent a copy to the S. of S. [Secretary of State]. (Diary 26.12.42)

The result came just a week later:

Saw CIGS, who, as I expected, tackled me on my recent letter to AG. He was very kind and concerned about possible effect on my career of reputation for being 'difficult'. He quoted my letter to R...and the fact that Eisenhower did not like me (which is mutual). My only regret is if I add to the worries of the CIGS. (Diary 5.1.43)

But, although BP would not admit it, the strain was telling.

Sinclair told me he could not understand how I managed to endure the frustration of the past 14 months; it was already beginning to get him down. But my temper has been much frayed in the process. (Diary 26.2.43)

On 15 September, Brooke commented in his diaries:

During the afternoon, I had a visit from Paget, who is not improving, and is, I fear, on the decline slope.

Fortunately, this turned out to be an unduly gloomy forecast, and BP was soon back to his usual determined approach to life.

I have travelled 81,000 miles in 12 months as C.-in-C., of which 24,000 were by rail, and the rest by car. This beats my predecessor's mileage by a handsome margin. (Diary 6.1.43)

A depressing feature of this period was that Home Forces had to supply a constant stream of trained reinforcements for overseas theatres, while they themselves had no operational role, except the defence of the UK, which was no longer a real challenge. It was difficult under these circumstances to maintain morale, (including that of the C.-in-C.) and BP wrote:

> The army at home has been set back a bit by the hurried creation of First Army, and no one gives a thought to the security of the UK.... What a grand army we could have, if up to strength and fully equipped.

The only operation for which Home Forces had to be ready at short notice, was an ad hoc return to Europe in the event of a sudden collapse by Germany, even though this was hardly likely. So BP's primary responsibility was the training of the forces for D-Day, together with the many problems of a growing presence of American troops in the UK, and the preparation for D-Day.

There was still complete uncertainty about who would be the higher commanders in the final stages of the war, and this was obviously of direct concern to BP. America was increasingly dominating the execution of the war, and the names of Marshall, Eisenhower and Bradley ran alongside those of Brooke, Alexander, Paget and Montgomery.

Then, on 6 March 1943, BP heard unofficially that he was to command 21st Army Group, the British element of the invasion forces and, on 5 May, he was officially confirmed in the rank of Full General. Finally, on 23 July, it was announced officially that he was to be C.-in-C. 21st Army Group, and the future seemed clear.

Notes
1. It was not however completely unprecedented, for a remarkably similar situation occurred in 1809, when the British Army in Portugal was evacuated from Corunna during the Peninsular War, and escaped to England to face the threat of invasion of England by Napoleon's triumphant armies.
2.. It was sent to Eastern and Southern Commands 'For Action', and 'For Information' to everyone else.
3. Alanbrooke noted later that on 17 May 1943 'Winston was in a bad mood, mainly owing to his dislike for Paget, and we got no further ahead'.

Chapter 6

Who Planned D-Day? (1942-1944)

Paget's SKYSCRAPER Plan has never been given the credit it deserves.

The Price of Victory. R.W. Thompson

It is an intriguing question. 'Who planned D-Day?' The generally accepted architect, and certainly the best known, is Lieutenant General Sir Frederick Morgan. He was responsible for all planning on behalf of the Allied Combined Chiefs of Staff (CCS) from April 1943 until D-Day on 6 June 1944; it was he who produced the final, successful D-Day Plan called OVERLORD, and who also wrote a book about it called *Overture to Overlord.*

But planning had, in fact, been going on since January 1942, when BP, as C.-in-C. Home Forces, was instructed by the British Chiefs of Staff to make plans for 'an opposed landing in France'. Work went ahead throughout 1942 and, on 18 March 1943, BP presented the Chiefs of Staff with a plan called SKYSCRAPER.

But just at that moment, it was decided by Churchill and Roosevelt that the planning for D-Day should be put into the hands of a joint Anglo-American staff under General Morgan. BP duly handed over a copy of SKYSCRAPER to Morgan, but to him it was just part of the 'mountain of paper that had accumulated over the years on the same subject'. He expressed his gratitude in his book for the preparatory work that he received from BP, but he did not mention SKYSCRAPER by name,[1] and as a result, it has remained largely unknown.

The remarkable feature about SKYSCRAPER was that it not only recommended the same landing areas in NORMANDY and the COTENTIN Peninsula that were eventually used on D-

Day, but it also proposed virtually the same invasion forces that finally took part (see the comparative table on page 71).

BP refused to raise the matter publicly in his lifetime, and so the story of SKYSCRAPER has never been fully set out. He did, however, feel strongly that the part that he and his staff had played in the D-Day planning should be properly recognized, not for personal credit, but simply to set the record straight. Now, sixty years on, I believe the time has come to tell the full story, as it appears in my father's papers and diaries.

Paget's Plan (SKYSCRAPER)

The story of D-Day planning begins with the meeting between Churchill and Roosevelt in Washington in December 1941 (code name ARCADIA). Despite the grim situation in the war at that moment the two leaders boldly agreed to plan for an invasion of Europe from Britain as soon as possible. As a result the British Chiefs of Staff issued a directive to BP as C.-in-C. Home Forces in January 1942

> ...to prepare an Outline Plan for operations on the Continent in the final phase, and to review the plan periodically with a view to being able to put it into effect if a sudden change in the situation should appear to warrant such a course.

The operation was called ROUND UP, and the planning naturally included all three Services. The other operational commanders in the UK at that time were Admiral Sir Bertram Ramsay, (C.-in-C. Portsmouth) and Air Marshal Sir Sholto Douglas, (C.-in-C. 2nd Tactical Air Force).[2] They were known as the Combined Commanders, and, together with Admiral Lord Louis Mountbatten (Combined Operations), they were responsible not only for D-Day planning, but also for a number of other operations that might be carried out from the UK.

During the planning that went on throughout 1942, it emerged that there were, among those involved, two different schools of thought as to how to tackle the problem. The first (the majority view) maintained that effective planning could not be carried out until it had been laid down at the highest level what resources would be available for the operation being considered.

The second (minority view) was that the resources required for the task could not be properly estimated except on the basis of some sort of plan. This was the approach that was strongly held by BP, and he worked on that basis. He had been given no guidance as to what forces might be available for the operation in question, or the landing craft available to transport them across the Channel, and he therefore went ahead on the basis of producing a sound plan, together with an assessment of the resources required to implement it.

In July 1942 plans for ROUND UP were complete, and were passed to the Chiefs of Staff, but they were rejected as being impracticable, and the project was abandoned. The question now was 'What next?' The answer was SKYSCRAPER.

Planning continued to be carried out by the Combined Commanders, based in Norfolk House in London, for a return to Europe. In November 1942 Major General Charles Loewen took over as BGS Plans under BP, and thus became the chief architect on the Army side of all planning for D-Day.

From the start it was an extremely frustrating business. There were endless vital questions to which an answer was required if realistic planning was to go ahead, and BP was constantly pressing the War Office on a mass of issues to which an answer was urgently needed, but could all too often simply not be provided. As late as March 1943, he recorded in his diary:

> I pointed out that delays and lack of decision were not the fault of the Combined Commanders, but lack of direction from the Chiefs of Staff. (13.3.43)

A month later he wrote:

> It is tragic that we can make so little progress, though we are quite clear as to what is needed. (19.4.43)

Although the planners had little information about the resources available, they did have plenty of data about the topographical factors and all-important information on matters

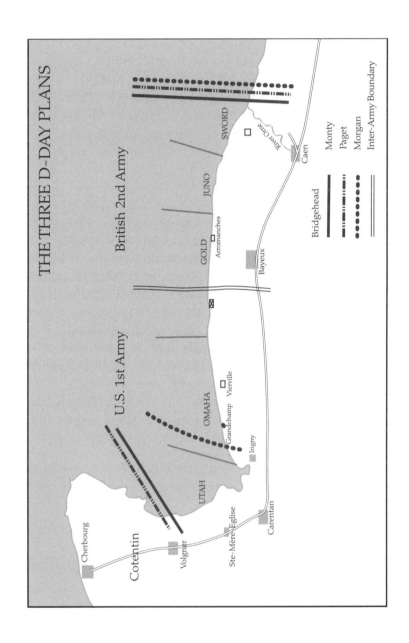

THE THREE D-DAY PLANS

such as tides, harbours, enemy defences, and airfield sites. But it was not just a matter of obtaining essential information. There was also the time factor; over 2 million men had to be trained for an unprecedented operation on an enormous scale with many risks and uncertainties. Realizing the impossibility of obtaining details of the resources available, BP and his staff resorted to the well-tried military method of an Appreciation of the Situation, and gave it the code name of SKYSCRAPER.

BP made it absolutely clear in the opening paragraph of SKY-SCRAPER what the aim of the paper was:

The object of this paper is to obtain decisions on certain major points which must govern not only planning for a return to the Continent against opposition, but more particularly the organization, equipment and training of the Army in the UNITED KINGDOM during 1943.

He then went on to give his outline plan. This covered the question of WHERE the invasion should take place, and on this point he was quite definite:

The study 'Selection of Assault Areas for a Major Operation in North West Europe'[3] has left a choice of one area only; the CAEN beaches, plus the East beaches of the COTENTIN Peninsula.

His assessment of the troops required was equally definite, and his plan envisaged:

a. Ten divisions afloat, of which three are required to seize and open CHERBOURG. (This was before Mulberry Harbours had been thought of.)

b. Three divisions for the assault on D-Day plus two more on D plus 1.

c. Four follow-up divisions, two landing on D-Day and two on D plus 1.

d. Four to five airborne divisions. He considered it essential to 'impose substantial delays on the arrival of enemy reserve division', and this should be achieved by air bombing, SOE and airborne landings.

61

The interesting point here is that the areas chosen for the landings on D-Day, and also the troops allotted to the invasion are virtually those that were finally agreed in 1944. (see page 71)

SKYSCRAPER was completed on 18 March 1943[4] and was passed on 22 March direct to the CIGS (some nine months before the final OVERLORD plan was agreed).

The reaction of the Chiefs of Staff to SKYSCRAPER reached BP on 5 April 1943, and to his surprise, it amounted to a complete rejection. The plan was described as 'far too general', and they declared that they found themselves 'unable to agree with the assessment of resources required'.

The final conclusion was that 'on the whole, in view of the fact that planning for definite operations is to be pressed forward, the further study of the general principles enunciated would be of only academic value'.

This verdict was greeted with considerable disappointment by BP and his planners, who found it hard to accept that the result of nine months of intensive labour was so summarily dismissed as 'of only academic value'. Even more serious from BP's point of view was the fact that he had not been given any of the crucial decisions that he had hoped for, to enable him to go ahead with the training, equipping and organizing of the Army that he commanded, and that would have to carry out the invasion.

But there was a reason for this lack of interest in SKYSCRAPER, although it had not been revealed to BP. The answer lay in the phrase 'Planning for definite operations is to be pressed ahead'. Indeed, it was already in hand, for it had been agreed at the conference in Casablanca in January 1943 that detailed planning for a joint Anglo-American cross-channel invasion should start as soon as possible, and that a joint Anglo-American staff was to be set up to implement this.

COSSAC

The stated aim of the new directive was 'to give cohesion and impetus' to the planning for D-Day, and on 1 April 1943 Lieutenant General F.E. Morgan was appointed as COSSAC, short for 'Chief of Staff to the Supreme Allied Commander'; the problem was that the Supreme Commander had not yet been appointed, and it was not even known whether he would be British or American.

On 13 April Morgan and his Anglo-American team officially took over responsibility for all D-Day planning from the Combined Commanders' Planning Staff, and BP was thereby freed from that particular commitment. He remained however C.-in-C. Home Forces, and as such, was still responsible for all the preparations for invasion.

Morgan's instructions came to him in a formal directive,[5] dated 23 April 1943, which made him responsible for planning three separate operations:

a. STARKEY A deception plan for invasion.

b. RANKIN A sudden return to France.

c. OVERLORD A full scale invasion of Europe against opposition.

The plan for OVERLORD was to be ready by July 1943. This was a formidable task, particularly as there was still no Supreme Commander to whom he could turn for decisions. Morgan was, as Robert Thompson put it:

…a man without a head to his body, without enough executive power, without enough troops or the craft to carry them.[6]

Morgan was given a copy of SKYSCRAPER on taking over, but, as he stated in his book *Overture to Overlord*, he found on arrival:

…a mountain of paper that had accumulated over the years on the same subject, tipped off by the work of a body known as the Combined Commanders, who had for some months been allotted the task of thinking up projects for a cross-channel assault.

He did, however, fully appreciate that a vast amount of valuable work had already been done:

The more we became aware of what had been done, the

more we came to realize that we were heirs to a considerable fortune...there was actually little that was needed of original work.

He also accepted that:

None of these past planners had enjoyed the advantages given, and to be given, to us. It seemed that they had in the main been asked to tackle the problem in a way which seemed to us the wrong way round. Starting with a blank sheet, so to speak, they had been asked to deduce what tools would be necessary to finish the job. Almost invariably they seem to have been told that while their plans, as plans, were fine, there was no prospect whatsoever of the resources needed to put them into effect being made available, so that either the first proposal must be varied or a new one must be thought up. This type of frustration is probably the worst of all.

It was a fair assessment of the problem that had faced his predecessor.

The COSSAC planners were indeed much better placed than BP's team. As Morgan put it again:

The question came to us quite differently. By early 1943, the output that would be available for 1944 could be reasonably assessed. We could therefore ask ourselves the question: 'With these tools, can the job be finished or can't it?' To this would have to be added, of course, the supplementary question 'If so, how? And if not, why not?'

It was a momentous question for any planner to have to answer, but fortunately, help was at hand. On 26 May 1943 COSSAC was given a supplementary directive by the Combined Chiefs of Staff which, in his words, 'got down to brass tacks'. It specified the aim to be to seize Continental ports, with a target date of 1 May 1944. For the first time, the resources available were stated, and the answer was a total of twenty-nine divisions for the assault and immediate build-up; of these, five divisions were to be loaded for assault, with two in the follow-up, plus two airborne divisions.

At last the planners had something concrete to work on, and, as Morgan put it:

All this pretty much completed our essential elements of information.

But time was short, and the problems to be tackled were formidable. He set to work, and again gave credit to his predecessors:

The majority of the ingredients had already by 1943 been painstakingly evolved as the result of immense labour on the part of a large number of people.... . In fact, had not planning and preparations been carried out for many months before the COSSAC organization was conceived, there could have been no possibility whatever of launching the operation in 1944.

It soon became clear to Morgan, however, that he faced the same two problems that had proved so difficult for BP. First, he still had no Supreme Commander, and second, there was still a continuing shortage of landing craft, which affected the number of troops that could be deployed.

Morgan also faced the further problem that, although he now knew the resources available, it became increasingly evident that these resources were not really adequate to the task that he had been given, and he would therefore have to cut his coat according to the cloth available.

The result was that he soon concluded that he must reduce the scope of the invasion plan, in order to make it a feasible operation with the resources allotted, and he therefore made the crucial decision first, that the landing could only be on a front of three beaches, and NOT the five proposed by BP in SKY-SCRAPER,[7] and second, that the COTENTIN Peninsula would have to be excluded from the initial assault area.

Morgan's Plan (Overlord I)

COSSAC submitted his plan to the British Chiefs of Staff on 15 July 1943 stating that, in his opinion, the operation was feasible by the target date of 1 May 1944 'given a certain set of circumstances in existence at that time'.

His plan envisaged an assault by three divisions with a follow-up of two divisions. The landing area was to be astride the VIRE Peninsula, with the aim of seizing the area within the line GRANDCHAMP – BAYEUX – CAEN – OUISTREHAM. This frontage was to be controlled by one corps headquarters. He estimated a built-up to eighteen divisions within two weeks, with a view to 'a thrust south-west to gain CHEROURG.' D-Day remained planned for 1 May 1944.

The main difference from SKYSCRAPER was that Morgan's Plan did not include the COTENTIN Peninsula in the initial assault area, primarily because he felt that it was not feasible with the resources available. He was also worried that the enemy could cut off the entire COTENTIN Peninsula, and he wrote late: [8]

> We could make our plan work if on D-Day there were not more than a total of 12 German, full-strength mobile field divisions in FRANCE.[9]

He added as his final verdict:

> I have come to the conclusion that, in view of the limitations imposed by my directives, we may be assured of a reasonable chance of success on 1 May 1944 only if we concentrate our efforts on an assault across the Norman beaches about BAYEUX.

Two other significant conclusions of Morgan's were:

> a. The objective of supreme importance is the town of CAEN with its command of communications.

> b. Any increase in resources should take the form of an increase in the planned rate of build-up, then expansion of the front of assault, first to the west and then to the east.

BP and the Combined Commanders' had both considered the COTENTIN Peninsula landings to be an essential part of a sound plan for the invasion, and this controversial issue of whether they should be included or not, would remain unresolved until December 1943 when Eisenhower and Montgomery arrived on the scene as the operational commanders and made the long-overdue operational decisions on these vital issues.[10]

In the absence of a Supreme Commander, the British Chiefs of Staff approved Morgan's Plan and, on 28 July, sent him to the USA to discuss it with the Americans. It was considered at the QUEBEC Conference in August 1943, and was finally accepted with few changes by the Joint Chiefs of Staff Committee, subject to the agreement of the Supreme Commander and his Deputy, when appointed.

A step forward was taken at the conference in Quebec in August 1943 (QUADRANT) when COSSAC was given a new directive. In the continued absence of a Supreme Commander, this made him not only responsible for all planning for the cross-channel assault, but also for taking 'all necessary executive action' to implement the plans. It was an improvement, but it still did not give him the power to make decisions which could only be the responsibility of the operational commanders concerned.

The move did however effectively end BP's involvement in D-Day planning but he still, of course, had the formidable responsibility of organizing and training all the Army troops involved, as well as having to be prepared to carry out a sudden invasion of Europe, if German resistance should suddenly collapse.

21st Army Group

On 24 June 1943 BP was officially informed that he had been selected to command 21st Army Group, the British element of the invasion force. It did not come as a complete surprise, because it was a logical decision, when he had been responsible for all the preparations to date. It was certainly regarded by most of those concerned as a right and proper decision, but BP himself was remarkably unmoved:

Received 'urgent memorandum' from the MS (Military

Secretary) dated yesterday, 'You have been selected to command an Army Group. Further details and the date upon which you will be required to assume duty will be communicated to you as soon as possible.'

I suppose I ought to be thrilled, but I am not. I do not feel it really gets us nearer to the invasion of the Continent, and I have no personal ambition.

He now joined Admiral Sir Bertram Ramsay and Air Marshal Sir Trafford Leigh-Mallory as one of the three Joint Commanders for the invasion.

All now seemed clearer, and on 7 December 1943 the Joint Commanders held their first meeting to discuss the Outline Plan. BP wrote in his diary:

> I was very temperate in stating my case for two armies carrying out the initial assault instead of one; the latter is mainly a political decision to balance my command of the whole operation, the idea being to have an American (Bradley) commanding one army.... Curious to note how much has been discussed and settled by COSSAC with Ramsay and Leigh-Mallory without reference to me.

He was right in his feeling that he was being left out of things, for this would in fact be the only Joint Commanders Meeting that he would attend. On 9 December he learned that he was not to command 21st Army Group on D-Day after all, but was to hand over to General Montgomery, then commanding the Eighth Army in Italy.

It was a bitter and unexpected blow, but all he wrote in his diary was:

> I gathered from the S. of S. (Secretary of State, Sir James Grigg) that Winston wants Monty to take over command of 21st Army Group from me. I can understand this and shall, I hope, hand over without bitterness.

There were many crucial changes taking place at this time. On 7 December Eisenhower was finally nominated as the long-awaited Supreme Commander, with Tedder as his Deputy.

Morgan was replaced as COSSAC by Eisenhower's strong supporter, Bedell-Smith, with Morgan agreeing to step down and becoming Deputy Chief of Staff to Eisenhower.

When Eisenhower studied Morgan's Plan, he was not at all happy with it, and told the Joint Chiefs of Staff that he would like to see a heavier initial assault on D-Day; as a result three more divisions were earmarked for the invasion by cancelling other operations.

On 1 January 1944 Monty arrived in England to take over 21st Army Group, and was immediately told by Eisenhower to study Morgan's Plan and give his views on it. He did so, and his verdict was equally critical:[11]

> The initial landing is on too narrow a front and is confined to too small an area... . My first impression is that the present plan is impracticable.

When he had had time to go through the plan in more detail, he declared:

> We needed an initial assault by a least five divisions, with additional airborne troops dropped on the flanks to secure us from flank interference, while we pushed quickly inland. We would need a build-up which would give us, say eight divisions on shore by the evening of D-Day, and twelve by the evening of D plus 2. (these figures to include airborne divisions). We should aim to have eighteen divisions on shore by about the end of the first week.

He went on:

> The more I examined the proposed tactical plan of the Army, the more I disliked it. The front of the assault was too narrow, only one Corps Headquarters was being used to control the whole front, and the area of landing would soon become very congested.

Eisenhower entirely agreed, and Morgan was ordered to revise the plan. But the lack of landing craft was still a serious problem if the scale of the initial assault was to be enlarged. After much debate, Eisenhower, as Supreme Commander, finally recommended that ANVIL (the Allied invasion in the South of France) must be postponed from May to August 1944, in order to make the additional landing craft available for D-Day. This was agreed, and it was also agreed that D-Day must be postponed by a month from 1 May to 1 June 1944.

Monty's Plan (OVERLORD II)

These crucial decisions meant that Morgan's COSSAC Plan could now be made into a practical proposition, and he promptly set about revising it on the new basis. On 21 January the new version (still called OVERLORD) was submitted to Eisenhower, who approved it.

Detailed planning now went ahead on the basis of the four major changes that had been made:

a. Two more divisions to be added to the assault on D-Day, making five instead of three.

b. The Cotentin Peninsula to be included in the D-Day assault area.

c. The additional landing craft required to be made available.

d. The assault to be controlled by two Armies instead of one.

The intriguing outcome of these changes is that they made the eventual OVERLORD Plan virtually identical to the original SKYSCRAPER Plan, in that all the above points had been included in SKYSCRAPER. They were not, however, feasible propositions when SKYSCRAPER was first presented, and so it was not surprising that the Chiefs of Staff rejected it in April 1943. What is most remarkable is that BP and Monty both in fact came up with virtually the same plan for the invasion – without ever meeting to discuss it! It says much for the value of Staff College training and for basic military Appreciations of the Situation!

The crucial differences were that Monty's Plan (OVERLORD II) was based on the premise that specific and adequate resources would be available and that it also had the backing of the commanders involved. Paget's SKYSCRAPER, on the other hand, had had to be planned *in vacuo*. Yet, in the end, the two were almost identical.

There were thus three plans for D-Day over the years:

a. Paget's Plan (SKYSCRAPER) produced by BP and his staff in March 1943 with no knowledge of the forces that would be available.

b. Morgan's Plan (OVERLORD I) produced by Morgan in July 1943, based on specific, but inadequate resources, as specified to Morgan.

c. Monty's Plan (OVERLORD II) produced by Morgan in January 1944, based on the increased resources considered essential and made available by Eisenhower and Monty.

It is interesting to compare the main features of each of the three plans:

	PAGET	MORGAN	MONTY
Date:	18.3.43	15.7.43	21.1.44
Assault Area:	Normandy and Cotentin	Normandy only	Normandy and Cotentin
Number of Beaches:	5	3	5
Assault divisions:	5	3	5
Airborne divisions:	4-5	2	4
Divisions afloat:	10	7	12
Army HQ	2	1	2

Post Mortem

In 1947 Morgan published his personal account of the planning for D-Day, entitled *Overture to Overlord*. The book was naturally eagerly awaited by BP and his staff, and it was with some surprise and dismay that they found that there was no specific mention of them as being involved in the planning. Morgan did give generous credit for the work that had been done before he took over,[12] but it was in general terms only. BP realized and accepted that SKYSCRAPER could not be mentioned by name, because at that time it was still classified Most Secret, but he felt strongly that Loewen and his team should have been given more credit for their achievement in the production of SKYSCRAPER, and he set about trying to put the record straight.

Loewen agreed with him about the remarkable similarities between SKYSCRAPER and OVERLORD II but said he was

> ...a bit shy of seeking to gain any particular credit for any of this.... 'Although I prepared the papers, it was you who accepted SKYSCRAPER as an expression of YOUR view as the Commander responsible, and submitted it, bearing all the responsibility'.[13]

In 1959 BP wrote to Lord Alanbrooke, who had been CIGS in 1943, to get his views on SKYSCRAPER, and received a reply, dated 12 March 1959:

> My dear Bernard, I found SKYSCRAPER most interesting, and a great similarity in this plan to that finally adopted.... It is a pity that the plan did not receive some recognition from Freddie Morgan, as it is certainly very similar to the final one in many respects. Yours ever Alan.

BP also wrote (on 23 May 1959) to General Ismay, who had been Secretary to the Chiefs of Staff at the time:

> If you have time I shall be very interested to know your reason for describing the plan as 'academic'. I promise you that it is not with a view to writing my memoirs, which I have no intention of doing. But I would like to give credit to

Loewen and his planning staff for what I regarded at the time, and still regard, as a remarkable achievement.

I have always wondered why you used that adjective 'academic' (referring to SKYSCRAPER), for my plan was very similar to that actually carried out, and is far better than Freddie Morgan's OVERLORD, which Monty rightly scrapped. I presume it was because at that time you saw no chance of getting the landing craft required for SKY-SCRAPER....

General Ismay replied on 8 June 1959:

My dear Paget, I am ashamed to confess that I only remember SKYSCRAPER as one of the many plans which did not materialize.... I am particularly astonished that I should have told you that the plan was 'academic'. It is not an epithet that I would have used, unless the Chiefs of Staff had positively directed me to do so.... I still cannot understand how SKYSCRAPER, which, as you say, was not unlike OVERLORD, could be called 'academic'. Surely, the answer of the Chiefs of Staff should have been 'This looks like a very useful paper, but planning for the return to France is now in the hands of an Anglo-American party under COSSAC. We are sure that they would find SKYSCRAPER a very valuable study'.... All I can say, with great sincerity, is that I am very ashamed at having used the epithet 'academic' – even if under orders from superior authority – without sending you a personal explanation at the same time. Yours ever Pug Ismay.

It was a generous answer, and BP felt much happier – even vindicated. But he still steadfastly refused to think of seeking public vindication, which he felt would involve controversy and hurt to others. Several friends urged him to put his side of the story, either by writing his memoirs or by allowing some writer to quote him (and there were several who would have been happy to do so). He did, however, assemble and keep what papers he could, so that historians would one day be able to pass judgement and they are the basis of this book.

He also sent a copy of SKYSCRAPER to Basil Liddell Hart, the outstanding historian and military analyst of the time, who wrote on 9 August 1960:

> Your papers on SKYSCRAPER go far to confirm what I had already gathered from other sources – that most of the key points in the final plan, which have been represented as radical changes, were not really new, and had already been foreseen.
>
> I was particularly interested in your idea of using the parachute troops more deeply and widely than was eventually done, to attack the objectives of the sea-landed reserves from the rear and to 'delay the enemy reserves'. It always seemed to me that the crux of the problem was to block the early intervention of the defenders 'counterattack' divisions. In that respect, and not on that alone, I think that your plan might well have proved more effective than the one that was carried out.

BP in turn replied

> … We attached special importance, as you did, to blocking the early intervention of the German counterattack divisions. I have very painful memories of how often we failed to do this in the Kaiser's War.

My father also wrote to me, having asked me for my views:

> You are quite right to describe the plan as a staff study. But you must take account of the particular and most aggravating problem which faced me early in 1943, which was to try to get the Chiefs of Staff to face up to the tremendous task involved in the invasion of NW Europe, and to put in hand the essential preparations. I have never in my life experienced a more difficult and frustrating experience.

Conclusion

The saga of the planning for D-Day seems to be a classic example of the two opposite approaches to the long-term planning of any major operation of war. The first option is to prepare the best possible plan, worked out on the known facts and factors, but not based on any specific resources being available to carry it out. This was the basis for SKYSCRAPER. The second option is a plan based on known resources. This sounds easier, but has the grave disadvantage that the allotted resources may not be adequate to achieve success. This was the case with the first COSSAC Plan, which had to be watered down, due to limited resources.

Another key factor that emerged was that all planners need a senior commander to whom they can turn for decisions on crucial issues and for support in obtaining essential resources. Neither BP nor Morgan had this support initially, and it was not until Eisenhower and Monty appeared on the scene in January 1944 that it was possible to match up the plans with the resources to implement them.

So, who planned D-Day? BP and his planners set out in SKY-SCRAPER what they considered essential for success, only to be told that their conclusions were 'academic'. Morgan was given limited and inadequate resources, only to be told that his plan was 'impracticable'.

So, it was back to Square One in both cases, but with the difference that, in January 1944, there was, at last, a Supreme Commander who could demand what he considered to be essential, and get it. On this basis, OVERLORD was finally worked out, and D-Day was successful.[14]

The saga is perhaps best summed up by R.W. Thompson in his book *The Price of Victory*, written in 1960:

> Paget's 'Skyscraper' has never been given the credit it deserves. It is uncommonly like the final plan for 'Overlord' adopted by Montgomery…the final plan remained fundamentally the creation of COSSAC, built upon the foundations laid by Paget. He had been forced to build with shadows, spinning invisible webs, and sustained by drive and faith. (page 261)

Notes

1. There was a good reason for this, in that Morgan wrote his book in 1947, and SKYSCRAPER was not downgraded from MOST SECRET to UNCLASSIFIED until 22 January 1959.

2. He was replaced later by Air Marshal Sir Trafford Leigh-Mallory.

3. CC (42) 108, dated 5.2.43.

4. HF/00/570/G. (Plans), dated 13.3.43.

5. It was 'commendably brief', covering merely a page and a half of foolscap.

6. *The Price of Victory*, page 89.

7. In the event, some 185,000 men, including 20,000 paratroops, landed on D-Day in 20,000 vehicles and 4,200 landing craft.

8. *Overture to Overlord*, page 162.

9. Stalin is said to have commented cynically 'What if there are 13?'

10. On 20 July Morgan dined with BP, who commented: 'F.E. Morgan came to dine and is in a depressed state of mind; he is now experiencing what the Combined Commanders had to put up with! I gave him a few home truths.'

11. *Memoirs*, page 219.

12. He wrote to BP in January 1944: 'As you have realized full well my job has not been easy, but I should like you to know that but for your help on many occasions, I am sure it would have been quite impossible.'

13. Letter to BP, 22.2.59.

14. Allied casualties on D-Day were around 2,500 killed (1,000 of them on Omaha Beach) compared with 20,000 British troops killed on the first day of the Battle of the Somme on 1 July 1916.

Chapter 7

Forging the Sword (1941-1943)

To Bernard Paget, who so well trained the soldiers that took part in this great adventure that, when the weapon was handed to me, it was easy to wield.

With my best wishes.
Montgomery of Alamein. Field Marshal.

When BP took over as C.-in-C. Home Forces in November 1941, he began what was probably the greatest achievement of his life, the three-fold task of first training the Army that would invade Europe on D-Day; second, forming 21st Army Group that would fight from Normandy to the Baltic; and third, maintaining morale in the Army at home during two and a half years of inaction and frustration from 1940 to 1943.

It was a formidable challenge and an undertaking on an unprecedented scale. Initially, in 1940 the task was to be prepared to defend Britain against invasion. Then, as this threat receded, it became a matter not only of training some 2.5 million troops in Britain, but also welding the many different forces involved, primarily British and American, but also Canadians, French, Belgians, Poles and others, into one integrated Army. It meant building up cooperation between the three Services to a degree never achieved before. At the same time Home Forces had to train and equip a constant stream of reinforcements for formations overseas that were already fighting the Germans, Italians and Japanese.[1] Finally, BP had to organize, equip and train 21st Army Group as a new formation and, at the same time, prepare detailed plans not only for D-Day, but also for a series of other possible operations.

A Common Doctrine

BP constantly preached the need for a common doctrine in training, which everyone in all three Services could and would follow. From 1940 onwards a new approach to all training, at least for the Army and its supporting Arms, was implemented throughout Home Forces, based primarily on Battle Drill, and taught through Battle Schools. This was developed by BP with great determination, and culminated in the creation of a School of Infantry, which remains today as the primary source of all Infantry training.

BP has justly been described as 'a second Sir John Moore', and it is an intriguing comparison. Both were Light Infantry soldiers, not only in fact, but also in spirit, and both produced a new concept of training for the Army of their day.

Sir John Moore created and trained the incomparable Light Division that fought so brilliantly throughout Wellington's Peninsular War from 1809 to 1814; he was killed at the Battle of Corunna in 1809, and so did not see his division in action during the rest of the campaign. BP likewise created and trained 21st Army Group, but was denied the satisfaction of commanding it in battle. He was to Montgomery what Moore was to Wellington.

Both of these imaginative leaders set up training schools. Moore's was at Shorncliffe in Kent, and BP's was at Barnard Castle in North Yorkshire. Both taught a totally new concept of mobility and initiative i.e. Battle Drill. Both achieved their aims through total dedication and an unwavering belief in their ideas against all difficulties and doubters. Both aroused in the hearts of their soldiers, whatever their rank, a fighting spirit that would carry them to final victory.

Realistic Training

Before 1939 training in the British Army had been anything but realistic; flags were used to represent tanks, and rattles signified machine guns; exercises were few and brief, and seldom involved any hardship or endurance. Financial restrictions ruled out the use of much ammunition, either live or blank, while restricted training areas, combined with strict safety regulations, prevented any useful realism. In BP's words:

> ...in peacetime we have an absurdly centralized and pettyfogging peacetime administration, imposed on us by our financial system...we suffer from the paralytic motto of 'safety first', which is the negation of sacrifice and service.

What would he say about the absurd 'Health and Safety' doctrine of today?

In 1940-41 the emphasis was inevitably on defence and survival, and priority had to be given to measures against the threat of invasion; as a result, no exercises took place above unit level. There was a chronic shortage of weapons of all sorts and virtually no ammunition was available for training; transport was limited, and so was equipment, with priority being rightly given to troops being sent overseas.

Another constant problem was the shortage of good training areas, where weapons could be fired, tanks driven and aircraft used; this was steadily improved, and by the end of 1942, some 6.5 million acres were available for training compared with 1.5 million pre-war.

In 1942 BP issued to all Commanding Officers some notes written by Lieutenant Colonel Stewart of the Argyll and Sutherland Highlanders about the Burma Campaign of 1941, to which he himself added the comment:

> He attributes our failure there, not to lack of equipment, but to the academic outlook of all ranks from general to private, which resulted in a lack of realism in training, and in everyone, commanders, staffs and units, being physically and emotionally surprised by the actual conditions of battle.

In November 1942 BP issued a pamphlet entitled *The Technique of Training*, which covered the principles involved at all levels from the individual soldier to divisional commanders. He emphasized the vital importance of initiative at all levels, but at the same time insisted on the need for a common doctrine. This is taken for granted today, but in 1941, with a rapidly expanding conscript army, it was the essential basis of all training.

BP insisted, like Sir John Moore, that two basic rules must be followed:

a. All training must be realistic, so that, in his words 'all ranks are physically and emotionally prepared for battle'.

b. All ranks, and particularly the junior leaders, must be kept fully informed at all times, and so be able to use their initiative when needed.

If a man in the ranks knows nothing of what is happening, he cannot be expected to play his part. (address to the GHQ Battle School. 26.2.42)

With memories of German air superiority in Norway still vivid in his mind, he insisted on the closest possible Army/Air cooperation on all training, with aircraft providing close support whenever available. But until 1943 there was little or no inter-Service training, and it was only after the disaster of the Dieppe Raid in August 1942 [2] that this was developed under the aegis of the Director of Military Training.

Infantry as 'The Cutting Edge'

One thing that BP was determined to eradicate once and for all was the image of the Infantry as 'the P.B.I.' (Poor Bloody Infantry). He expressed his views very clearly to the School of Infantry on 17 August 1942.

The opening of this Infantry School will, I believe, prove to be a very important event in the history of the British Army through the assistance it will give in raising the status of the Infantry and in establishing a common doctrine for the Infantry, which is essential for effective cooperation. As regards our status, that should never have been in doubt. But up till recently, we have suffered from the effects of the last war with its trenches and its barrages; we have been treated like P.B.I. and used as a labour exchange by the rest of the Army. We are now in the process of establishing that we are in effect the principal arm, and we shall prove it, as we have so often done before, in skilled and stubborn fighting. As we all know, a higher standard is required of Infantry in skilled and stubborn fighting than of any other arm.

He was fond of quoting Field Marshal Wavell's well-known comment that 'it is the platoon and section commanders of the Infantry who do most to win our battles'. And, in September 1944, he had a pamphlet issued entitled *The Status of the Infantry*, which made absolutely clear the importance he attached to them as the 'cutting edge'.

BP regularly complained that whereas the RA (Royal Artillery), RAC (Royal Armoured Corps) and the RE (Royal Engineers) all had a capital letter to their title, the infantry had to suffer the indignity of a small 'i' ! Moreover, while there was a Major General, Royal Artillery, a Chief Engineer and a Director of the Royal Armoured Corps, the Infantry had no one to represent them! It was a tremendous satisfaction to him therefore that he was able to put this right when in 1942 he created the first ever Major General of Infantry. (see page 83)

He made his views absolutely clear in an address to the GHQ Battle School on 26 February 1942:

...You and those whom you are going to teach here have a great opportunity and a great responsibility, namely to re-establish the forgotten fact that the Infantry is the principal arm in winning battles, and that in this, the British infantry is second to none.

BP was not always so complimentary when inspecting training, and he would always speak bluntly, allotting criticism or praise as he felt necessary:

I still see far too many flagrant and unnecessary examples of lack of realism in our training.

The divisional attack was an awful reversion to 1917-18, a 'funeral march' of P.B.I. behind a so-called barrage. Must put this right. It is the Divisional Commanders who are chiefly to blame. (Diary 16.9.43)

Battle Drill

Battle Drill was the basis of all infantry training during the war, and it has continued as such ever since. It incorporated all the principles in which BP believed so strongly, and it also provided the Common Doctrine that he wanted. Indeed, it will always be associated with him, and so it is worth telling more about it.

The first idea of Battle Drill emerged in 1940 soon after Dunkirk, and was the brainchild of Major General Harold Alexander, Irish Guards, then commanding 1st Division. He wrote a paper on the subject, and set up a training school in Ashdown Forest to put his ideas into practice in his own division. Training began at unit level, and continued progressively up to divisional level.

It might be expected that General Alexander, being a Guardsman, would be unduly influenced by 'barrack square drill', but this was in no way the case. His concept was carefully designed to broaden the discipline of 'barrack square drill', and adapt it to the conditions of modern warfare. The dominant theme was 'Fire and Movement', linked with 'Flexibility' and for a start, everything was done 'at the double'. 'Initiative' was demanded from everyone, and, combined with Guards' discipline, this produced results.

Sir John Moore must have looked down with considerable approval to see his 'light infantry' tactics being revived in this way – and by a Guardsman at that![3]

BP first encountered Battle Drill when he visited the Battle School being run by Major General J.E. Utterson-Kelso for his 47th (London) Division in August 1941. BP, with his 'light infantry' mind, immediately saw the potential[4], and his enthusiasm was kindled. From then on he supported the concept in every way he could, with the result that every division in Home Forces was soon setting up its Battle School.

Not surprisingly, BP saw merit in a GHQ Battle School, and he discussed the idea with Utterson-Kelso, who wrote to him on 22 January 1942:

General Sir Bernard Paget GCB, DSO, MC, DL as C.-in-C. Home Forces, 1945. (*By courtesy of the RGJ Museum Trustees*)

Bernard's mother, Helen, with her six children at Christ Church, Oxford, in 1897. Left to right: Beatrice, Edward, Helen, Humphrey, Frida, Richard and Bernard.

The four brothers at Cuddesdon, 1910. Left to right: Richard, Edward, Bernard and Humphrey.

Captain Bernard Paget, Adjutant, 5th Battalion Oxfordshire and Buckinghamshire Light Infantry, 1915.

BP in Quetta in 1936 as Commander, 4 Infantry Brigade.

The German delegation at the funeral of King George V in January 1936, with BP in charge.

The opening of the Senior Wing of the Staff College at Minley Manor on 21 January 1939. BP, as Commandant, chats to HRH The Duke of Gloucester and to the CIGS, General Lord Gort, VC.

BP on a visit to the Oxfordshire and Buckinghamshire Light Infantry at Bulford on 10 April 1943, when C.-in-C. Home Forces.

BP at his desk as C.-in-C. Home Forces.

Lieutenant Anthony Paget, younger son of BP, who was awarded an Immediate DSO for his gallantry, fighting with the Oxfordshire and Buckinghamshire Light Infantry in Germany in March 1945. He died of wounds in another engagement shortly afterwards.

The author, then Adjutant, 3rd Battalion Coldstream Guards, stationed in Palestine, visited his father at Headquarters Middle East in Cairo in 1945.

Badges of formations
in Middle East
Command in 1945.

Titles of formations
in Middle East
Command in 1945.

G.H.Q.

MIDDLE EAST

ARMIES.

8.   9.   10.   12

CORPS.

10.   13.   25.   30.   I Aus.   21 Ind.   3.   2 Polish.

DIVISIONS.

2 Amd.   10 Amd.   8 Amd.   I Amd.   7 Amd.   6. S.A. Amd.   N.Z.   6 Aus.   70.   9 Aus.

1 S.A.   2. S.A.   50.   7 Aus.   44.   51.   5.   56.   4.   46.   78.

1.   4 Ind.   10 Ind.   5 Ind.   6 Ind.   8 Ind.   31 Ind. Amd.   3 Carpathian.   5 Kresowa.   7 Polish.

INDEPENDENT ARMOURED BRIGADES, ETC.

4 Amd.   7 Amd.   8 Amd.   23 Amd.   I Amd. Bde. Gp.   23 Amd. Bde. Gp.   9 Amd. Bde. Gp.   I Army Tk. Bde.   32 Army Tk. Bde.

231 Inf. Bde.   L.R.D.G.   Force 281.   3 Ind. Mtr. Bde. Gp.   252 Ind. Amd. Bde.   38 Ind. Inf. Bde.   I Gr. Bde. Gp.   2 Gr. Bde. Gp.

Pol. Amd. Bde.   I B.M.C.B.   Jewish Bde.   M.N.B.D.O. 2.   F.F.L.   Belg. Congo Bde.   Raiding Forces.

COMMANDS.

B.T.E.   Troops Aden.   Troops Sudan.   Palbase.   P.A.I.C.

AREAS.

Cairo.   Canal.   Alexandria.   A.I.F. Base Area.   88.

T.J.F.F.   Iraq Base.   Northern Area.   Tripolitania.   Cyrenaica.   21.

ALLIED HEADQUARTERS.

N.Z.   Australia.   Yugoslav.   Polish.   Greek Army.   B.M.L. Greece.   Arab Legion.

BP with the CIGS, General Sir Alan Brooke, and Nahas Pasha, Prime Minister of Egypt.

Field Marshal Montgomery visits the Middle East just before taking over as CIGS.

BP with Emir Abdulla of Jordan.

BP with Glubb Pasha (wearing forage
cap) who commanded the army of the
Emir of Jordan, the Arab Legion.

BP with Field Marshal Smuts, for whom he had a great admiration.

Edward Paget, Bishop of Southern Rhodesia and Chaplain General to the Rhodesian Forces, visits Cairo and preaches in the Cathedral to his younger brother.

BP with his old friend, the historian, Arthur Bryant, who dedicated his book, *Years of Victory*, to BP.

The liberation of Rhodes in 1945. BP accompanied the Greek Regent, Archbishop Damaskinos, on a triumphant drive round the island.

A dramatic, historical pageant in Athens Stadium on 15 May 1945 to celebrate the liberation of Greece, attended by over 100,000 people.

Greek guerrillas, with their leader, Colonel Zervas.

Children of members of the Polish Army make a presentation to BP, who had a great admiration and affection for the Polish forces in the Middle East.

A farewell inspection of his Regiment at Osnabrück on 14 October 1955. Behind BP is the Commanding Officer, Lieutenant Colonel Tony Read, together with BP's successor as Colonel, Major General Sir John Winterton. The Warrant Officer on parade is Regimental Sergeant Major John Stevenson, DCM, a distinguished figure in the Regiment.

As Colonel of the Oxfordshire and Buckinghamshire Light Infantry, BP hands over the old Queen's Colour to the Dean of Christ Church for safe keeping on 8 May 1955.

BP as Governor of the Royal Hospital Chelsea, escorts the Inspecting Officer, Field Marshal Lord Alexander, on Founder's Day 1957.

BP takes his last salute from his Regiment at Osnabrück on 14 October 1955 at a parade to mark the bicentenary of the forming of the 52nd in 1755. With him is Major General Sir John Winterton, his successor as Colonel.

General Sir Richard Church, Commander-in-Chief of the Greek Army in 1826, wearing the Evzone uniform. He was the great-great-uncle of BP.

BP at his home in Petersfield in 1957 with his wife, Winnie, and his brother, Edward, recently retired from being Archbishop of Central Africa.

BP with his granddaughter, Olivia, in 1958.

I do not want any recognition or renown. I only want our nation to survive this war. If at any time you were to feel that you wanted me at your GHQ Battle School, I would be prepared to give up my Division, and descend to any rank dictated by the Auditors – and to come and give a hand.

BP did not accept the offer, but did even better by appointing him as the first-ever Major General of Infantry, a decision that proved both momentous and highly successful.

In January 1942, the GHQ Battle School was opened at Barnard Castle in North Yorkshire and, on 26 February, BP visited it. In his address, he related how he had obtained the backing of the Prime Minister to the concept of Battle Drill:

I will tell you how the GHQ Battle School came to be created. Some time ago, the Prime Minister circulated a note in which he said that renown awaited the commander who succeeded in re-establishing the efficiency of artillery against tanks.

I challenged him on this, and said that I thought even greater renown awaited the commander who restored the role of the Infantry as the principal arm in battle. He asked me to send him a paper on the subject, and I sent him one written by General Utterson-Kelso developing this idea, which had decided me to create a GHQ School of Battle Training.

The PM, in his capacity as Minister of Defence, cabled to me from America to say that he thought the paper admirable, and that I could count on his assistance in every way in putting it into practice, and that he would do his best to ensure that the Infantry should no longer be considered as a 'labour exchange' for the rest of the Army.

He ended with:

While I greatly admire the conception of a well-armed Infantry Battalion working with the élan and combined individualism of a pack of hounds, I am also anxious about the smart side of things. I hope there are going to be no fussy changes in the Manual Exercises, and that 'spit and polish' will not be incompatible with effective field training.

BP was happy to reassure the Prime Minister on both the last points!

In March 1942 BP took the unprecedented step of inviting a group of editors from the national newspapers to the GHQ Battle School at Barnard Castle to show them what was being done, and how his training methods could help to win the war. One of them was Frank Owen of the *Evening Standard*, and he wrote:

> I saw today the most inspiring sight in England since the broken remnants of the Luftwaffe went trailing home in September 1940, thrashed out of our skies by the boys of the RAF...
>
> I saw a band of brothers, happy, resolute and utterly confident that they will make this Army the finest sword in the world. By Heaven, they will do it.

BP also took the presence of the press as an opportunity to attack one of his 'pet hates'. He told them:

> Commanders have to spend far too much time meeting the demands of an absurdly centralized and pettifogging peacetime administration imposed on us mainly by our financial system.

It worked, and Frank Owen was happy to offer supporting fire:

> ...the whole British Army is going to school but this magnificent New Model Army of ours is gasping for breath under a deluge of paper.... Ask any single divisional commander what is his greatest curse, and he will unhesitatingly reply 'I am occupied in filling in forms with names and numbers, instead of filling human hearts with the fire of battle'.

Times do not change. What would they say today? Probably the same as the famous broadside by the Duke of Wellington during the Peninsular War:

If I attempted to answer the futile mass of correspondence that surrounds me, I would be debarred from all serious business of campaigning. As long as I hold an independent position, I shall use my utmost endeavour to ensure that my officers are not prevented by the scribbling of mere quill drivers from attending to their first duty which is the training and care of the private men under their command.

BP too had clear cut and emphatic views on such matters, and above all, in his praise and admiration for the Infantry:

...we have in the British soldier the finest fighting man in the world, but there must be leadership to make the best of his qualities. (Address to the School of Infantry, 17.8.42)

On 27 August 1942 he wrote in his diary:

Battle Drill training has produced remarkable results on infantry training, and CIGS said I had made revolutionary progress in the Army by getting it going.

By October 1942 BP was in a position to claim in a talk to the Staff College:

Every Division now has its Battle School where battle training is taught and exercises carried out using all the Infantry weapons, and tanks, and aircraft when available, under realistic conditions.
...I believe that the results of this realistic training and battle inoculation will prove to be one of the major lessons of this war, and I cannot emphasize too strongly the effect it has had on the troops under my command. (Diary, 3.11.42)

It was no idle boast, and it was reinforced by one of the Divisional Commanders concerned, Major General Thomas, who commanded 43rd Division from 1940 to D-Day and wrote in the divisional history:

C.-in-C. Home Forces...introduced the rigorous, realistic training which alone offered any prospect of success. Efficiency in battle overrode all other considerations...the

Division came to accept hardship as the natural order of things.

BP believed in seeing things for himself, and he much enjoyed getting away from his office and the War Office, and instead, visiting units all round the country. After a visit to 43rd Division in 1943, he wrote:

Much impressed by the quality of training and intelligence of all ranks during my two days with 12 Corps. Am told how glad the troops are to see me. I equally get great uplift from meeting and talking to them, and I feel much more at ease with them than in Whitehall. (Diary, 15.12.43)

But BP continued to put his message across on every possible occasion and, on 25 April 1943, he recorded:

A very successful two days at the School of Infantry, attended by all Army, Corps and Divisional Commanders...remarkable unanimity among all the higher commanders present that the methods demonstrated are correct, and that the term 'P.B.I.' no longer applies.
...Have arranged with the DMT (Director of Military Training) for all Infantry Brigadiers and Commanding Officers of 21st Army Group to attend a similar, short course at the School of Infantry, followed by a refresher course for all Company Commanders, this will, I believe, establish the doctrine.

Battle Drill was undoubtedly proving a success, but there was the occasional problem. In May 1942, the emphasis on building up an effective fighting spirit got out of hand in some quarters and developed into the so-called 'hate training', as some over-enthusiastic instructors at some Battle Schools encouraged an attitude of 'hate' for the enemy.

There were public protests, and BP had to have a meeting with the Bishop of St Albans, who had raised the issue. As a result, a letter was sent to all Army Commanders banning the use of strong language on training, and any attempts to arouse blood lust or 'hate' as part of training. BP described it as 'a complete negation of leadership...and any attempt to raise it by artificial means is bound to fail.

He added 'When such language is used by NCOs to officer students, I consider that it is harmful to discipline.'

There is a good story (reported in *The Times* of 25 November 1941) of one Battle School which ran a course for, among others, all the Regimental Sergeant Majors of the division. *The Times'* War Correspondent was invited to attend, and he wrote:

> For the first few days the RSMs sulked superciliously, it is said, but then became so enthusiastic that one of them (formerly a Sergeant Major of the Guards at that!) actually offered the suggestion that all polished brasses should be coated with khaki paint.

Discipline and Morale

One of BP's great achievements, in addition to the training of the Army, was, first, the raising of morale after the setbacks of Norway and Dunkirk, and then the maintenance of morale during two and a half long years of inaction and frustration. It was a daunting task under such circumstances, but it was done. He did not hesitate to set out the challenge facing the Army:

> What are we up against? The best disciplined, the best trained and the toughest military power the world has ever seen, and a people possessed by the spirit of sacrifice for an ideal. But we can win on all these points, if we are determined to do so, and possess the necessary inspiration.

As a Regimental soldier BP believed unreservedly in the vital part played in morale by the well-proven Regimental system, and by Regimental officers and NCOs:

> It reflects great credit, especially on Regimental officers, that morale has been maintained and strengthened throughout this long wait without the stimulus of battle. I am very much impressed by that fact as I go round the Army, and I do not believe that any other Army in the world could have

succeeded in this difficult and trying phase. (Talk to the School of Infantry. 17.8.42)

In another talk to the GHQ Battle School in 1942, he made the same point:

In all wars morale has been a very important factor…. In this war the German technique had been to undermine the enemy's morale before attacking suddenly and in great strength…the maintenance of our determination and our morale is therefore a vital part of our war effort …. Since Dunkirk we have been called upon to show a different and more difficult form of courage than courage in battle, which is to remain confident and cheerful without the stimulus of battle for a long period of time, with little apparent incentive and little hope of glory. That the Army has succeeded so well in this very severe test reflects the greatest credit upon all concerned and especially upon the Regimental officer.

He then turned to the question of discipline:

Discipline must be closely related at all times to fighting efficiency, since its main purpose is to foster 'esprit-de-corps', which will hold men together as a team and see them through the test of hard times. If a man has a proper pride in his Regiment and in his Division, he has the greatest incentive to discipline, courage and endurance…we must make every effort to avoid boredom and monotony in our training…which must be based on the principle that periods of intensive training, calling for effort, endurance and the acceptance of risk, are alternated with short periods of relaxation, during which great attention should be paid to comfort and welfare.

Above all, I look to all Commanders for inspiration by personal example, and the setting at all times of the highest possible standards of Duty. Let us remember that we are fighting the war NOW.

Such words set out very clearly BP's personal belief – and they have a remarkable relevance still today sixty-five years on.

It is interesting that BP always spoke of 'Discipline and Morale' together, linking them as being mutually supporting and associated. An outward expression of this was the emphasis that he placed on the importance of saluting which he saw as a gesture not of subservience, but of mutual respect.

There was a story that another general remarked upon the exceptionally high standard of saluting in one division that he visited, and he was told 'Ah. But General Paget was here a few days ago.'

BP set a remarkable example himself of both discipline and morale. His self-discipline and dedication can fairly be described as amazing. A sixteen-hour day was routine, and it was a non-stop day too; he wanted to see everything for himself and visit every unit, be it an Army Education Centre or a Commando unit; he inspected the cookhouse as much as the weapons and the assault course. He covered over 80,000 miles a year visiting troops and watching training; he might visit three or four units in a day, watch exercises of all sorts and sizes, and have endless interviews with generals, cooks, clerks and fighting men. He gave many talks, which were always stirring, though he said he found them difficult and 'they do not come easily to me'. Then it was back to GHQ with piles of paper, problems and people.

He was sustained in this punishing routine by the genuine stimulus and satisfaction that he got from meeting his troops, face to face, particularly the other ranks. On one visit he recorded: 'A real tonic to visit such first-class troops. I feel I could do anything with them.' Consciously or not, he was echoing the Duke of Wellington who said much the same of his Peninsular Army in Spain.... 'I could do anything with this army.'

Battle Drill in Civilian Life

There was no doubt about the value of Battle Drill in war, but it is of interest to note that there was at least one example of the same principles being applied just as effectively in civilian life. An officer in the Coldstream Guards called Major Cuthbert Fitzherbert was Chief Instructor in the Guards Training

Battalion at Pirbright from August 1942 to May 1944. He was sent on a course at Barnard Castle in November 1942, and was deeply impressed.

As a result he wrote later:

> During the course great emphasis was laid on the necessity that all ranks should know what is the purpose in hand and the means of achievement. I went back from this course feeling that I took away with me something that I should keep throughout life.
>
> I re-designed the training programme at Pirbright to conform to the School of Infantry doctrine, and the response from young officers, NCO's and Guardsmen was immediate and striking. It was, in fact, a clear result of both leaders and led having a common purpose, and of speaking the same language. I shall never forget my feelings when I saw that the charm had worked, and realized that it was a simple matter, based, as it was, on the most commonsense foundation.

After the war, Fitzherbert became a Director of Barclay's Bank, and was responsible for helping some 6,000 members of staff who had been in the Services to re-adjust to the challenges of peacetime. Applying the principles learnt at Barnard Castle, he and the other Directors worked out, first what the staff would want to know, and should know, about civilian life, and second, what they could usefully be told about the bank and its policies to enable them to adjust and play their part.

Fitzherbert then wrote to BP to tell him all about it:

> Having ourselves worked out both the questions and the answers, the Chairman sent out a series of letters to all concerned, setting out the bank's policies and how they affected the staff.... We have designed Refresher Courses for all returning warriors, and made them compulsory.... Our decision is based on two main reasons. Firstly, we want to ensure, as far as possible, equality of opportunity, and secondly, we hope that by passing the majority through the

same process, we will given them all something of the spirit that has worked so well elsewhere.

Barclay's Bank were extremely pleased with the results achieved, which were impressive, and BP was delighted by the vindication of his beliefs in civilian life as well as in the Army.

Verdicts

The final verdict on BP's achievements from 1940 to 1943 was the successful landings by 21st Army Group on D-Day, followed by the campaign from Normandy to the Baltic. It was the work of one of the finest armies in our history, created, by a strange coincidence, by two outstanding soldiers, both called Bernard, both sons of bishops and both worthy of the title of 'Crusader'.

The verdict of the historians was unanimously one of respect and admiration.

R.W. Thompson wrote in *The Price of Victory* (page 163):

Montgomery inherited a magnificent army from General Paget, highly trained and reinforced throughout by hard cadres of experienced troops. Its morale was high. It knew exactly where it was going and why…they had great faith in themselves and their commanders…they were ready to go.

Montgomery sent a copy of his book *From Normandy to the Baltic* to BP, and in the front he wrote:

To Bernard Paget.
Who so well trained the soldiers that took part in this great adventure that when the weapon was handed to me, it was easy to wield.
With best wishes. Montgomery of Alamein. Field Marshal.

BP described this as 'a very generous tribute'.

In August 1945, the great historian, Arthur Bryant, paid a visit to the School of Infantry at Warminster, and wrote to BP in Cairo:

It would move you to hear how they speak to you. I shall

always think of Barnard Castle as a dream come to life, a dream of what an army might be, and ought to be…. And one of the instructors remarked 'How I wish the Chief could drop in and see the result of all his hard work and fighting.

Brigadier H.W. Houldsworth, who was Commandant of the School of Infantry 1943-44, wrote to BP in 1944:

I would love to show you the mass of letters from ex-instructors and students, who have written to me and others here, thanking God for the teaching they got while they were here.

Basil Collier declared in *The Defence of the UK* (pages 297-8):

In every theatre in which British troops went in action, the great importance of Paget's contribution should not be forgotten.

Ian Hay wrote in *Arms and the Men* (pages 162-3):

It was for his work in forging the weapon which pierced Hitler's Western Wall that General Paget will chiefly be remembered, though fate denied him the final honour of wielding the weapon himself. As a trainer of troops and organizer of victory, he performed the same service (on an infinitely greater scale) for Alexander and Montgomery as that rendered by Sir John Moore to Wellington, and his name will be honoured by all soldiers accordingly.

On 14 March 1945 the Secretary of State, speaking in the House of Commons on the Army Estimates, referred to comments made by Montgomery about the troops of 21st Army Group, then fighting in the Reichswald:

All ranks were imbued with that infectious optimism and offensive eagerness which come from physical well-being, and from a firm belief in a just and righteous cause…. It was a great inspiration to see such fine soldiers ready and anxious for battle.

The Secretary of State then went on to ask:

How many people realized how much of the credit for this was due to the hard and unremitting work of General Paget in earlier days. The Field Marshal did. (Cheers.)

BP's personal comment, written in a letter to me on 27 March, was typical:

I wish I could stop all this reference to my training of 21st Army Group. P.J. Grigg referred to it in his Estimates speech. It does no good, and some people might think I was jealous of Monty, which I am not. I fully realize that he is better qualified than anyone else for the vast job he is now tackling so well.

Notes
1. The total amounted to 102,000 trained troops sent overseas in drafts in 1942 alone. In addition, Home Forces also dispatched elsewhere: five infantry divisions, one armoured division, one independent brigade group (address to the Staff College, 3.11.42).
2. There is no mention anywhere in BP's diaries of the Dieppe Raid.
3. My father, as a dedicated Light Infantryman, enjoyed referring to me, serving in the Coldstream Guards, as a 'heavy-footed-, flat-footed Guardsman!'
4. 'A first-class show, run by officers under 30 and fanatics in their beliefs; work is thoroughly realistic and makes physical demands on those attending. Battle Drill is the basis of the training; saw an excellent demonstration of a platoon in attack, using live ammunition dangerously.'

Chapter 8

21st Army Group
(June – December 1943)

Taking Over

When BP took over command of 21st Army Group in June 1943 it consisted of the three armies that were at that time earmarked to carry out the invasion of Europe; they were Second (British) Army under Lieutenant General Dempsey, First (Canadian) Army under Lieutenant General Crerar, and First (US) Army under General Bradley. Home Forces, now under General Franklyn, continued in its role of organizing and administering all the Allied forces in the UK, as well as providing reinforcements for formations overseas.

When BP was officially informed on 23 June that he was to command 21st Army Group, his only comment was:

> I suppose I ought to be thrilled, but I am not. I do not feel it really gets us nearer to the invasion, and I have no personal ambitions. (Diary, 24.6.43)

The *Daily Mail* however on 20 August wrote:

> As a future leader of a group of armies the claims of General Sir Bernard Paget are outstanding. For some time now he has been at work in the capacity of C.-in-C. Home Forces, first of all in defending Britain against invasion; and secondly, changing over large armies from the defensive to

the offensive. (*Who Will Lead us into Europe?* Lieutenant Colonel T.A. Lowe)

On 17 August BP was promoted to substantive Full General, with effect from 5 May 1943, although he had held the rank since December 1941.

As a balance to the fearsome responsibilities that he now assumed, there were some compensations that he much appreciated. He already had his invaluable, official train 'Rapier', and now Sir Michael Bowater most generously presented him with 'a magnificent Rolls Royce for my official use'. He used them both regularly, and on one occasion when watching a Combined Operation exercise in Scotland, he also spent some time aboard Lord Mountbatten's[1] private yacht, after which he commented:

I feel it is high living to travel by special train, luxury yacht and Rolls Royce, but I shall still take kindly to my bicycle when the time comes. (Diary, 19.8.43)

A major concern to BP (and to many others) at this time was who would be the Supreme Commander for the invasion. BP would have liked to see Brooke in the post, but a factor against that was that, because of the ever-increasing proportion of US troops involved, it was more likely to be an American. Meanwhile it was extremely difficult and frustrating for BP and everyone else to be in the dark on this vital issue, and on 25 September he wrote complainingly:

CIGS tells me nothing…maybe they have someone else in mind for my job. (Diary, 25.9.43)

Handing Over

In fact, he was nearer the mark than he thought, for 'they' had just decided at the Quebec Conference in August 1943 that there should be a major reorganization of higher commanders, as part of which BP would be replaced as C.-in-C. 21st Army Group by General Montgomery, then commanding Eighth Army.

Brooke knew well how hurtful this news would be to BP, because he had himself just learned that he too was to be disappointed in his hopes. Churchill had earlier promised him the post of Supreme Commander, for which his claims were outstanding, but now it was not to be:

A dark cloud of despair descended. It was a crushing blow. He offered me no sympathy, no regrets at having had to change his mind, and dealt with the matter as if it was of minor importance. (*Alanbrooke Diaries*, page 442.)

On top of his personal disappointment, Brooke now had to sort out the implications of the changes for others, including BP:

The replacement of Paget with Montgomery for the liberation of France was a matter which was causing me much anxiety. Since the threat of invasion had lapsed, Paget had been placed in command of the forces in this country destined ultimately for the cross-channel operations. He had done a marvellous job in training up these forces, and I wish it had been possible to leave him in command for D-Day.

I had a great personal admiration and affection for him, which made it all the more difficult to have to replace him at the last moment. He had, however, had no experience in this war of commanding a large formation in action; his abilities, in my mind, suited him better for the duties of Chief of Staff than for a Commander.

Finally, I felt it was essential to select some general who had already proved his worth and in whom all had confidence. I had selected Monty for this job in my own mind, but I thought I might have trouble with Winston and Ike (or Marshall) who might prefer Alexander. Meanwhile P.J. Grigg (Secretary of State), who had a great admiration for Paget, was pressing for his retention, and although I was in complete sympathy with most of his feelings, I knew I must press for the appointment of Monty. (*Alanbrooke Diaries*, (page 454)

The first that BP heard of these changes was on 9 December, when the Secretary of State warned him unofficially that he would have to hand over to Monty. That night BP wrote in his diary:

culty – and it has been your show. But in addition, to have trained them to such a pitch, and on extremely modern lines, has been the greatest achievement of all. Whatever the future may bring you, you will have the satisfaction of knowing that you forged the weapon – even though others may use it.' (General Sir Archibald Nye. VCIGS, 18.1.44)

I was truly sorry to hear that after all you were not to lead 21st Army Group, and I know you well enough to realize that the decision will be a serious blow to you.... I feel for you very much, though I know better than some that you are a big enough man to stand the disappointment. (General Sir Charles Loyd, 12.8.43, GOC Southern Command and former Chief of Staff to BP.)

How magnificently you take your orders. What an inspiration! May we prove not unworthy of this partnership. (John C.H. Lee, Major General, US Army, 28.12.43)

This must be the most difficult moment to part from the Army Group you have done all the spade work to build, organize and train. I can say feelingly 'I'm sorry', and that conveys a soldier's understanding. (General Johnson VC, 28.12.43)

A compliment that BP particularly appreciated came in a letter to the *Sunday Times*, on 21 April 1946:

...I am an ex-ATS.... I travelled in the special train waiting on General Paget with another girl. He was a fine man, and everyone loved him. It was a great sorrow for all of us when he said 'Goodbye' one Christmas before he went to the Middle East.... We shall never forget the perfect gentleman, General Paget. (Mrs Nelly Miller, Kingsway, Hove)

Typically, BP not only acknowledged every letter, but also found time to write personally to the Manager of LNER who ran 'Rapier', and also to the Station Master at Barnard Castle, to thank them for the help they had given him while he was C.-in-C.

A final tribute worthy of being mentioned came in a book *The Watery Maze* by Bernard Fergusson (page 307):

Paget, an austere Cromwellian and dedicated soldier, had brought to a high pitch of training the British divisions (taking part in D-Day), and it was the cruellest of luck that he should now be relegated to preside over the faded glories of GHQ Middle East. But it was inevitable that a commander with recent laurels should be preferred, which meant in practice either Alex or Monty.

Note
1. Director of Combined Operations.

Chapter 9

The Middle East (1944-1946)

The extent of my command is considerable, it is more than 20 times the size of the UK, and twice the size of British India.

(BP talk to senior officers in MELF.)

Arrival

BP arrived in Cairo on 8 January 1944, not bitter, but deeply disappointed at his fate. He had been summarily removed from command of 21st Army Group, just when he expected to lead it into battle, which would have been the ultimate fulfilment of his career. Instead, he found himself in a non-operational command, where he and everyone else would have to watch history being made elsewhere. They were 'out of the hunt', and no longer had the overriding purpose of taking part in the invasion of Europe. He faced, once again, the problem of maintaining morale, just as he had in Home Forces.

> I do feel very lonely here, and rather depressed. My job is an anti-climax to 21st Army Group, and I feel all here are suffering from a sense of being 'out of the hunt'. (Diary 12.1.44)

His personal answer was to bury himself in his work, and he soon made his usual personal impact on those around him. He cut the routine staff meetings (known as 'Morning Prayers') from one a day to two a week,[1] and at the same time set in motion steps to reduce the strength of the headquarters by 22 per cent. Within a week he had demanded a paper from his

Chief of Education on 'The soldier's outlook and the problems of the Middle East'. A purge began of those who were not up to the mark:

> Must get rid of I.... He gets on my nerves.
> Saw F. and told him I would get rid of him if he failed to keep fit.

He personally worked to a fearsome schedule, driving himself to the limit, with no relaxation either on or off duty.

A Vast Command

As BP himself explained in a talk to senior officers, he was responsible for a vast area, with many, varied commitments:

> The extent of my command is considerable. It is more than 20 times the size of the UK and over twice the size of British India. From the Northern boundary to the Southern boundary the distance is 2,400 miles, while from Algeria in the West to the borders of India is 2,700 miles.
>
> Its composition is rather complicated. It includes four Commands – Egypt, Palestine, the Levant and PAIC (Persia and Iraq); there are also independent Districts and Areas of the Sudan (including Eritrea), Tripolitania and Cyrenaica, while Aden is partly my responsibility. There are, in fact, no less than 14 Governments...and 14 Codes of Law and no two of them are the same. Ration strength is constantly changing, but is currently about 850,000...this total includes troops of 36 nationalities, and 164,000 German and Italian prisoners of war.

There are three main threats to security:

a. Arab nationalism

b. Jewish nationalism

c. Xenophobia'

BP faced many remarkably varied problems, both military and

political. Militarily, there was the difficulty of maintaining morale in a non-operational theatre, where there was no obvious military objective, as there had been in the UK. The main operational problem in the Middle East came from civil unrest and also terrorism, and the emphasis, therefore, was on internal security, which soon became of major importance.

Most of the problems were political, and there were many potential trouble spots, where although the issues were essentially political, the results of any decisions taken, either military or political, would probably lead to a need for military action. They included:

Palestine	Egypt and the Canal Zone
Syria and Lebanon	Greece
Tripolitania	Persia and Iraq

Conversely, any military action was almost certain to have political repercussions of some significance, as for example, in Palestine, and it was essential therefore that civil and military worked closely together.

BP did not find this easy. First, he had, like many military men, a deeply engrained distrust of politicians. He blamed them for many of the problems of the Services, such as the country's unpreparedness for war in 1914 and again in 1939, for their lack of care of the troops after any war; for a failure to understand the significance of the Regimental system, and for many unwarranted financial restraints. He questioned their honesty, and suspected them of putting self-interest before the needs of their country. Indeed, he more often than not prefaced the word 'political' with the adjective 'damned'!

In the Middle East there was another controversial issue, in that BP felt strongly that the 'damned politicians all too often failed to stand up for British interests'. On 20 September 1944 he wrote to the ACIGS to complain:

British policy in the Middle East is not based primarily on British interests. We appear to be sacrificing our interests in Syria and Lebanon to the French, in Palestine to the Jews, in

Egypt to Nahas[2] and we have already sacrificed them in Saudi Arabia to the Americans…

His own view was uncompromising:

It is essential for Britain to cease trying to placate other people, including the Americans and Russians, and to be truly Britannic.

It was clearly not going to be easy for him to reconcile his robust, straightforward beliefs with the subtler, long-term thinking of the diplomatic mind, but he knew it had to be achieved, and that civil and military must somehow keep in step, understand each other, and together find the best answer. This was the main challenge that would face him on many fronts over the next two and a half years.

BP did not particularly enjoy life in Cairo, apart from his work.

I find Cairo social life excessively dull, and doubtless, they say the same of me.

He also found the work depressing:

There never seems enough time to get through my work here; the visitors are far more numerous than with 21st Army Group, and there is also more paper.

He had many duty engagements:

Have been invited to dine with King Farouk…. Very long drawn out and too much to eat, followed by a soirée; very good acrobatic team. Mlle… (supposed to be the best singer in Egypt) sang for half an hour; very monotonous, but the King thoroughly enjoyed it.

His main relaxation was a round of very gentle golf on the Gezira course, early in the morning; his opponent was usually his Director of Public Relations, Brigadier Pat McCormack who, after a year of this, solemnly presented BP with a large alabaster vase, inscribed 'The Commander-in-Chief's Cup. To be won by the Commander-in-Chief daily.'

BP embarked on a punishing, non-stop schedule of work, and drove himself to the utmost. On one day in March 1945, for example, he carried out twenty-one inspections, ranging from a general hospital to an African troop canteen and a repertory theatre. In one period of eleven months he flew 60,000 miles in his official plane 'Rapier'.

His Chief Medical Officer told him he should slow down, because he did 'far more than any ordinary man could compete with'. But he took no notice, remarking in his diary, 'I have never admitted to being tired.' He did however admit that 'I must curb my temper.'

The Greek Army Mutiny

It was not long before BP faced his first challenge, and it took the unexpected form of a mutiny. Greece was at this time occupied by Italy, and the Free Greek Army was based in the Middle East Command. It consisted of 1 Greek Mountain Brigade in Egypt and 3 Greek Mountain Brigade in Lebanon, and BP therefore became *ipso facto* Commander-in-Chief of the Greek Army. This was a remarkable instance of history repeating itself, for BP was himself a direct descendant of another British General, Sir Richard Church, who had been C.-in-C. of the Greek Army during the War of Independence (1821-1827).

On 6 April 1944 1 Greek Mountain Brigade mutinied. This was a direct result of Communist subversion, and so was very much a political, as well as a military problem, and BP kept in close touch with Churchill as to how to handle it. It was settled with no loss of life, except one British officer killed, and BP received Churchill's congratulations for his 'firm and well-considered action'.

The story is intriguing, particularly in view of BP's personal links with Greece, and it is therefore covered in more detail in Chapter 10.

In October 1944 BP was appointed as Extra Aide-de-Camp to the King, a special honour, because it was the personal gift of the King, and was in his case approved without waiting for a vacancy to occur. BP wrote to his wife that 'this is the only honour that I have really coveted'.

One of the more uplifting aspects of his position was meeting many VIPs who passed through Cairo and talking to them. Churchill was a regular visitor, as was General Brooke, the CIGS. Another welcome guest was his true friend, P.J. Grigg, the Secretary of State, for whom he had great respect, and to whom he could, and did, talk freely.

One of BP's favourite visitors was Field Marshal Smuts, whom he much admired, and whose wisdom he greatly appreciated. They were united in their belief in the need to stand up for British interests in such matters as the evacuation of the Suez Canal, to which Smuts, like BP, was strongly opposed. Both were dedicated 'imperialists'.

On 24 April 1944 BP recorded:

> Smuts told me he did his best to persuade PM to leave me with 21st Army Group, but now he thinks I may have a bigger job to do here, and that Providence has sent me to do it.

A year later Smuts visited Cairo again:

> He spoke impressively of the difficult times that lie ahead and of the vital need to uphold the British Empire, which is the wisest, most experienced and most humane of the three major groups of Powers. He said the task of reconstruction is far more difficult than after the last war. (Diary, 2.4.45)

A particular personality in the Middle East, with whom BP had frequent contact, was General Glubb Pasha, who commanded Emir Abdullah of Jordan's Arab Legion, a fine fighting force. Glubb was even more highly respected in the Arab world than Lawrence of Arabia, and he did have some perceptive views on Middle East affairs. He, like BP, saw the great possibilities of a Middle East Confederacy with a common strategic policy but he was also convinced, to his great regret, that there was little hope of reconciling such a concept with the existence of a State of Israel in the Middle East.

Perhaps the greatest boost to BP's morale came, as in Home Forces, from any visits that he could make to the troops. This was a world that he knew and loved, far removed from the complexities and frustrations of politics, and the tedium of office work. An example of how much he enjoyed this was a visit on 12 January 1945 to the barracks in the Sudan of the Duke of Cornwall's Light Infantry:

A really first-class show run on pre-First World War standards of Regimental esprit-de-corps.... Went on to see Sudan Defence Force doing an exercise in hunting 'Shifta' (insurgents). Travelled by car, horse, jeep and Shanks's Mare during the exercise. Lunched with Boustead and wished I could be a Company Commander here with the job of chasing 'Shifta'!

In the same year he paid a visit to his own Regiment, The Oxfordshire and Buckinghamshire Light Infantry, and inspected the 52nd:

Very well turned out Guard. Was introduced to Company Commanders and saw some training. No doubt about 52nd being outstandingly efficient, and still retaining the title of 'A Regiment never surpassed in arms, since arms were first borne by men'. I thoroughly enjoyed my visit.

Such approval was, however, far from automatic, and even the 52nd would not have been allowed to 'get away with' any failings! The verdict after any such inspection was often 'a good show', but it might equally be 'a poor show', or even 'a very poor show. The CO must go'.

At all times BP placed the greatest emphasis on the welfare of the troops, and he made this a top priority.

Wherever I go, I chase up the standards of living, in the Army, which are far too low. (Diary, 1.4.44)

His attention to detail was striking, and after one visit to Cyprus, the *Cyprus Post* referred very accurately to his 'penetrating questions and determination to see everything for himself'. He personally selected items of furniture for barrack rooms and canteens; he ordered wireless sets for isolated units and pyjamas for leave centres, and obtained a special issue of 4,000 tons of potatoes a month (a luxury in those days of dehydrated potatoes!), and commented, 'This should please the Troops'.[3] Extracts from the censorship reports showed that his efforts did have an effect, one soldier describing him as 'a fine chap as regards the welfare of the lads'. When told of this, his comment was:

I do not record this in a spirit of vainglory, but in thankfulness, that I am able to inspire such feelings in the Troops.

He placed equal emphasis on welfare in the wider sense, as he made clear in a talk to the staff of the Middle East Welfare Training Centre, which he had set up:

I set so much store by the work that you do.... Welfare work has nothing to do with charity...it is an effort to make life more worth living in the sense of stimulating mental and physical occupations, in helping other people to help themselves...and in generally widening their outlook and interests...your work is the basis of good management and a most powerful influence in raising and maintaining a high morale.

The Years of Victory

On 17 January 1945, the distinguished author, Arthur Bryant, arrived in the Middle East on a lecture tour; he was a true friend and an admirer of BP, and brought with him a copy of his latest book, *The Years of Victory*, which he had dedicated to BP with the words:

For Bernard Paget, who, like Sir John Moore, trained a British Army for Victory.

Under this he wrote:

From his grateful friend, the author, for whose benefit he made patent the grandeur of character and nobility of the British soldier.

It was a very fine tribute, and BP wrote:

> This is the highest compliment I have ever had paid to me. He gave me a number of appreciative letters he has received from all sorts of people, including Queen Mary, Baldwin, Oman, Trevelyan…and one from Field Marshal Lord Milne, who wrote, 'Dear Mr Bryant, may I, as a total stranger, but a great admirer of your writings, thank you for your generous acknowledgement in your last book of the great work done for the country by Bernard Paget, shoved into the background, because he was a too honest gentleman. Your analogy is interesting.I hope your next book will be *Years of Achievement.*

An old friend, General Sir Walter Braithwaite, wrote to BP:

> I envy you the dedication in Arthur Bryant's book…. I wish I could have achieved work which would have inspired an author of Bryant's brilliance to compare me with Sir John Moore in so few words and with such truth as he does Bernard Paget…. My best congratulations on a well-deserved tribute.

Personal Tragedy

A personal worry for BP at this time was that both his sons were on active service in North-West Europe. His elder son, Julian, was Adjutant of the 5th Battalion Coldstream Guards in the Guards Armoured Division, and his younger son, Tony, was a Platoon Commander in the 43rd, having followed BP into his Regiment.

On 4 March 1945 BP received a personal telegram from Monty in 21st Army Group:

> It is with great pleasure that I tell you I have today awarded the Immediate DSO to Tony…for his very gallant leadership in the Reichswald Forest on 16 Feb. Hope you are well. Great events are taking place here.

Citation

The citation for Tony's DSO read:

On the night of February 16 1945, 'B' Company, 43rd Light Infantry were ordered to capture the Asperberg feature and farm buildings outside the Reichswald and known to be held by the enemy. Lieutenant Paget was commanding No. 14 Platoon – one of the two platoons ordered to carry out this task. The assault was to be made behind a barrage across about 400 years of open ground, and was carried out with great dash in the teeth of enemy machine-gun fire which the barrage had failed entirely to quell. During this assault Lieutenant Paget's platoon captured four prisoners and two machine-guns, killed four Germans, and themselves suffered six casualties, including the platoon sergeant.

On reaching the objective Lieutenant Paget started to get himself firmly established. The enemy, however, men of the 2nd Parachute Regiment, were determined to hold on to this position – it was subsequently learned that they had been ordered to hold on at all costs to cover the withdrawal of a pocket farther north – and fought back with fanatical fury. The first step was to clear the farm buildings. Lieutenant Paget left two sections to cover the main exits, while himself with the remaining section set about clearing the buildings; as he entered the house the enemy fired a panzerfaust at his party, killing the section commander, wounding one man, and throwing Lieutenant Paget to the ground; at the same time another party of enemy attacked the two covering sections. Lieutenant Paget, with the remains of his assaulting section, killed all the five members of this new enemy party and returned again to clear the house. This he did, killing and capturing six Germans.

Fresh enemy attacks were made, and a party of nine Germans, each armed with spandaus, were all personally killed by Lieutenant Paget from behind a hedge; another party, however, succeeded in entering the house and were not finally mopped up until 7 am on the following day. Meanwhile the sergeant commanding No 15 Platoon had been wounded and Lieutenant Paget assumed command of both platoons and firstly established them. Both 38 wireless sets were knocked out and the company commander was killed in trying to establish contact with the position. First light found both platoons firmly on the objective with 16 prisoners and 34 Germans dead on the field. Lieutenant Paget by his undaunted leadership, sheer bravery and skill in the fight won a memorable battle, and contributed in no small measure in lightening the task of another formation advancing from the north.

Tony's DSO was indeed a most gallant feat which must have come very close to warranting a VC. But only four days after the news of the award reached BP came the message that he had hoped he would never receive. Tony had been wounded in the head in another battle on 24 February, and had died of his wounds twelve days later on 7 March. He was only twenty and this was the third time that he had been wounded in nine months. In that time he had been Mentioned in Dispatches, and awarded the *Croix de Guerre* in Silver, the only such award achieved by his battalion.

His death was a most bitter blow, and BP wrote in his diary:

The world will never be the same without him, but all the happiness we have shared and his love will remain with us.

He wrote to Winnie:

To me Tony is now the supreme example of courage and sense of duty.... What wonderful tributes his generation have paid to him, and how precious these tributes are, expressing as they do, the truth, simplicity and frankness of youth. They bring me great consolation, as I hope they do to you, because they all prove what a tremendous influence for good Tony's life and example have been.

As in 1944 when he was removed from 21st Army Group, BP now hid his deep grief by burying himself in his work, and in May 1945, a crisis blew up in the Middle East that would keep him fully occupied.

Syria and Lebanon (May-June 1945)

Peace in Europe came in May 1945, but it did not bring peace to the Middle East, where trouble developed on several fronts, as growing Arab nationalism challenged the status quo. Within weeks of VE Day, a political crisis blew up in Syria and Lebanon (otherwise known as the Levant), and firm military action was called for.

Syria and Lebanon had been administered by France ever since the First World War under a mandate from the League of Nations, which required them to 'enact measures to facilitate their progressive development towards independence'.

In 1940 both countries were seized by Vichy France and occupied, but they were liberated by the Allies in 1941. Britain then supported their claim for full independence, while at the same time admitting France's 'special position'. The French, however, although officially recognizing the independence of both countries, were reluctant to lose their influence in the area, and did little to make independence a reality. As a result, considerable resentment built up against the French and the troops that they still maintained in the Levant.

Under the Lyttleton-de Gaulle Agreement of 1941, the French retained the right to enforce law and order, if, for any reason, Syria and Lebanon proved unable to do so. But the same Agreement also recognized BP as the Supreme Commander in the Middle East, which meant that he was ultimately responsible for law and order in the Levant as part of his command.

> The French cannot increase their garrison without my permission. I have already told General Humblot (French Commander in the Levant) this, and he did not contest it. (Diary, 10.10.44)

In November 1943 there was serious rioting in the Levant against the French control, and as a result all the great powers confirmed the independence of Syria and Lebanon. But the French still refused to hand over control, in particular, of the *Troupes Speciales*, the locally raised troops whom they used to enforce law and order. They also refused to agree to the arming of the Gendarmerie, which BP considered was essential if they were to do their job properly.

A further crisis arose on 17 May 1945 when the French cruiser *Jeanne d'Arc* arrived in Beirut with 700 Zouaves aboard. These were assumed by the Levant States to be reinforcements for the French troops in the area, and there were widespread demonstrations, which the police and gendarmerie were unable to control.

On 19 May, BP wrote:

It seems almost inevitable that there will be a blow-up in the Levant, for which the French will be entirely to blame. I go there tomorrow and will speak my mind to Humblot (French commander in the Levant) and, I hope, to Beynet (French commander in Lebanon). But as far as doing anything is concerned, my hands are tied.

He duly flew to Beirut, and had talks not only with the French generals, but also with the Syrian and Lebanese Governments and the British officials there; he then visited British troops in the area.

On 28 May, he recorded:

I had a personal telegram from the Prime Minister approving my policy of strict neutrality. I hope he will alter it to something more dignified soon.

But the very next day, there were more disturbances, and the French claimed the right to intervene to restore law and order; there were clashes between French and Lebanese troops, and the French also bombed and shelled Damascus, causing considerable damage and some civilian casualties.

BP now reckoned that the only solution was for him, as C.-in-C., to intervene and take overall control of the situation, and he wired the CIGS accordingly.

On 31 May he finally got orders from the PM to take over and restore order. His plans were already made, and on 1 June he flew into Beirut with an appropriate show of strength. He had an escort of Spitfires, and also two destroyers were waiting in the harbour; he drove off, with an escort of armoured cars, and flying the Union Jack on his own car.

He went straight to see Generals Humblot and Beynet, and personally handed them their orders. All firing was to cease forthwith, and all French troops were to be withdrawn to their barracks.

> They seemed almost relieved to hand over responsibility, and did not object to my instructions…(Diary 1.6.45)

At the same time BP moved units of 31st Indian Armoured Division and an infantry brigade into the troubled areas; they deployed at 1300 hours, and by 1830, order was restored. The French complied with his orders, and the situation seemed under control.

BP then toured the area, visiting the British units and seeing the damage done; he covered 950 miles by road in 44 hours, and was warmly welcomed by the Lebanese:

> At Hama we left to a 'feu de joie' from the Bedouin, fortunately up in the air! Feeling is very bitter against the French, because of the bombing…. I consider that we intervened only just in time to prevent widespread troubles in the Middle East. (Diary 2.6.45)

An uneasy truce followed, but on 3 June came a report that more French troops were on their way by sea:

> If true, this is sheer madness on the part of de Gaulle Admiral[4] and I concerted plans to prevent any landing, either by persuasion or by force. (Diary 3.6.45)

On the 4th came a telegram from the PM, ending 'Your greatest triumph would be to achieve a peace without rancour'.

In the end, the French reinforcements did not arrive, and the tension eased. The Lebanese were delighted by events, and regarded BP as their liberator. Indeed, they wanted to name a street in Damascus after him, but he diplomatically declined the offer. He did however, accept a gift of a ceremonial dagger 'for my bravery and wisdom'.

The Saudi-Arabian Government also thanked him formally for his action, and BP replied by asking them to do all they could to restrain the Syrians and Lebanese from any provocative action in future.

The PM sent him a telegram to say:

> You have acted with great propriety and discretion, and you have my approval for everything you have done.

On 11 June BP flew back to Cairo, leaving comparative peace in the Levant. There then followed, not a rest, but ten days that well illustrate the incredibly hectic pace of life that BP faced, the remarkable pressures of his job, and the wide range of problems and responsibilities that had to be dealt with.

14 June   Attended the King's Birthday Parade in Cairo.

15 June   Flew to JERUSALEM for meeting with GOC (Lord Gort). Heard that three mortar emplacements with bombs in them had been found just in time, aimed at the saluting base where Lord Gort stood on the King's Birthday Parade. Discussed action to be taken in PALESTINE in view of the very tense security situation.

16 June   Flew to BEIRUT for a further meeting with General Humblot and Beynet. Found them friendly, and they expressed their appreciation of our personal relations.

17 June   Flew to DEIR EZ ZOOR to visit 31st Armoured Division. Back to BEIRUT for another meeting with Beynet and then Shone (British Minister).

18 June   Flew to PERSIA [where British troops were protecting the supply route to Russia]. Inspected a hospital, two camps and a Headquarters. On to HAMADEN for night. Lovely hollyhocks growing in cornfields.

19 June   250 mile drive to KAZVIM (?) to meet Russian general. All very friendly. On to TEHERAN to British Embassy to discuss defence of oilfields.

20 June   Toured hospital. Lunch party at Embassy to meet Americans, Russians and Persians. Had an audience with the young Shah, and was impressed by his sincerity and high ideals; was in full sympathy with his well-nigh impossible position. Meeting at Embassy to discuss withdrawal of British troops, summer camps, release of internees and defence of oil fields.

21 June   a.m Inspection of troops. p.m. by train to ANDIMISHIK (?)

22 June   Arrive DOUID (?) 0630. Inspected two camps and two hospitals. Temperatures up to 123 degrees.

23 June   By road to visit oil fields at ABADAN and elsewhere. Temperature 123 degrees again.

24 June   Took off from ABADAN at 0700. Reached CAIRO 1415. A lot of paper waiting.

It had been what even BP called 'an exacting tour'.

Middle East Confederacy

One crisis had been dealt with, but many more potential troubles remained, both military and political, and BP had to be prepared to deal with:

a. Rising Arab nationalism.

b. Egyptian demands for the withdrawal of British troops from Egypt.

c. Egyptian claims on the Sudan.

d. Arab hostility to any State of Israel.

e. Jewish terrorism in Palestine.

f. Continuing resentment in Syria and Lebanon against France.

g. The constant threat from Russia against the Middle East.

h. British strategic interests.

These issues were all very complicated, and it is not intended here to try to analyse them or to pass judgement on the rights and wrongs in each case. The aim is simply to give a broad-brush picture of the issues, in so far as they affected BP.

In the face of these many problems, BP developed the concept of a new approach to British foreign policy in the Middle East, which he called 'a Middle East Confederacy'. He outlined it to senior officers in the Command in August 1945:

I suggest that, in the face of the growing demands of nation-alism, not to mention xenophobia, in the Middle East, we are unlikely to get what we require in the way of security for British interests by the old-fashioned methods of bargaining and treaty negotiations with individual States. In the past we have based our demands for operational facilities, such as the defence of the Suez Canal, primarily on the needs of British security, and it has worked out alright in this war. But it will be much more difficult now to obtain any facilities which seem to infringe the sovereign rights of the State concerned.

If, on the other hand, we adopt a different line of approach, and, instead of basing our demands only on British interests, we base them on the demands of the Middle East as a whole, then I believe we shall have a better chance of getting what we want. The States in the Middle East would feel that they have a common interest with us, as we have with them, in providing for the security of the Middle East as a whole, including that of individual States. In fact, we would then be applying the principle of the unity of the Middle East.

The Canal has ceased to be our most important defence commitment in the Middle East, and we are now concerned with the whole area, and beyond it, to secure our imperial

117

communications by air as well as by sea, and also our oil interests.

In 1945 he submitted a paper to the Foreign Office and the CIGS, and on 30 August he had a personal meeting with the Foreign Secretary (Ernest Bevin) on the subject:

> I spoke of my views on a Middle East Confederacy, which he said appealed to him.... He intends to set up a strong economic organization in the Middle East....He does not favour partition for Palestine, but the bi-racial solution....

On 3 September Bevin wrote to BP, thanking him for his paper, which he said was 'very useful'.

BP returned to Cairo, and with the blessing of Bevin, set out to present his ideas personally to the key figures in the Middle East. He had meetings with King Farouk of Egypt, King Ibn Saud of Saudi Arabia, Emir Abdullah of Jordan, the Regent of Iraq and General Glubb Pasha. He received a generally favourable response, but with two strong reservations. First, all the rulers were concerned about the threat posed by the reactions of the Russians; second, they were all firmly opposed to the prospect of a State of Israel in the Middle East.

There were voices of dissent too from within the Foreign Office, but on 19 March BP had another meeting with Bevin:

> Went to the Foreign Office 1530 and had half an hour with Bevin...he was very interesting about his ideas to make the Indian Ocean into a 'British lake' in lieu of the Mediterranean, and getting South Africa and Australia to play their part.

But nothing definite materialized as far as a Middle East Confederacy was concerned, and BP heard no more. On the bottom of Bevin's letter to him of 3 September he wrote cryptically 'Nothing came of this'.

Palestine

Meanwhile, BP had to deal with the every day problems of his Command, dominated by two long-standing issues, Palestine and Egypt. In order to understand the complications of Palestine, it is necessary to know something of the background.

Palestine has been an issue in the Middle East ever since the Balfour Declaration of 1917, in which the British Government promised the Jews 'a home in Palestine'. After the First World War Britain was given a mandate by the League of Nations, under which she became responsible for the future of the country while the conflicting issues were sorted out.

It was a thankless task, for the entire Arab world in the Middle East was deeply opposed to the proposals from the start, and in 1936 there was an Arab revolt in Palestine with angry attacks being made on British troops. Thereafter the Arab leaders based their opposition to the proposal on a British White Paper of 1939 which stated that an independent Palestinian State should be set up, and that the British Mandate should be ended.

The Jews, however, demanded the implementation of the Balfour Declaration of 1917, and a Jewish Agency Declaration of 1942 further demanded that the British White Paper should be scrapped, and Palestine should become a Jewish State. The two viewpoints were diametrically opposed and irreconcilable – as indeed, they still seem to be today!

A key issue in 1944 and thereafter was Jewish immigration into Palestine, which was still Britain's responsibility under the mandate. The Holocaust and the plight of the Jews at the end of the Second World War led to demands by the Jewish Agency for an increased quota, but this was fiercely opposed by the Arabs and was not approved by Britain. As a result, there was large-scale illegal immigration, which soon became not only a security problem, but also a cause of growing Arab resentment.

The British troops in Palestine found themselves unpopular with both sides; the Arabs were bitter that Britain was letting in too many Jews, while the Jews protested that they were not letting in enough. Israel sought to achieve its aim of a recognized Jewish State not only through diplomacy, but also by terrorism, and on 6 November 1944, Lord Moyne, the British Resident Minister in Egypt, was assassinated by two Jewish terrorists in Cairo.

The outrage provided a good example of the complicated relationship between civil and military. Any potential political moves, such as restricting Jewish immigration or closing down the Jewish Agency, would have immediate military repercussions, with which BP would have to cope and he did not have enough troops to do so. Equally any precipitate or mistaken military moves could well make the whole situation worse, both military and politically.

Throughout BP's time in Cairo, the Jews waged a ruthless, sophisticated terrorist campaign against British forces in Palestine, and it remained a major security problem. It was almost inevitable that BP would himself become a target for the terrorists, and sure enough, it was discovered that he was on their 'assassination list'. But, to his indignation, he discovered that he was Number 2, with his Chief of Intelligence as Number 1!

He was told that he must have two permanent bodyguards, who were to accompany him everywhere, even when he was playing his golf. He nicknamed them 'Trigger' and 'Safety Catch', and tried on several occasions to be rid of them, but without success.

Egypt

Another escalating problem was Egypt, where there was a growing demand for the complete withdrawal of British troops from the country. The situation here was governed by the Anglo-Egyptian Treaty of 1936, under which Britain had agreed to withdraw her troops from Egypt in due course, except from the Canal Zone, where we maintained the right to retain forces for the defence of the Suez Canal.

The Treaty was subject to review after ten years i.e. in 1946, but by 1944 Egypt was not only demanding an earlier review, but was also making further demands for three so-called 'national rights'. These were:

a. The total evacuation of British troops from the whole of Egypt.

b. Egyptian control of the Suez Canal.

c. The union of the Sudan with Egypt.

The British Government proposed accepting the first demand, for a complete evacuation, in the hope that this would lead to more goodwill in the future from the Egyptians, and a more favourable attitude to the other two demands. BP however disagreed strongly with this proposal, and he was very much supported in this view by Field Marshal Smuts.

> I told him that my view was that to offer the Egyptians complete evacuation would be disastrous to British interests and prestige. He agreed strongly, and wholeheartedly condemned what he called 'a policy of scuttle'. It was a great tonic to hear him talk. (Diary 24.4.46)

BP was always glad to see Smuts, and found in him a kindred spirit with whom he could discuss the problems of the rapidly changing post-war world. He had a very real respect for the views of a great statesman who appreciated the difficulties that BP had to face.

Despite his protests, BP was ordered to make plans for a withdrawal from Egypt, and he did so; but he wrote a strong paper[5] at the same time opposing the proposal and suggesting an alternative. In April 1946 a delegation from the UK, under Lord Stansgate, came to Cairo, to conduct negotiations with the Egyptians, and BP was naturally closely involved. But the proceedings were not to his liking:

> I have not yet heard any one of the Delegates speak of British and Dominion interests, except myself.

At the instigation of the Foreign Office, he requested an audience with King Farouk to state his case, and they had a meeting:

> He was very friendly and obviously out to cooperate. He said he had agreed to see me, because he knew me well and appreciated my broad-mindedness. He is well informed and seems to have a good Intelligence Service.

But the meeting did not change the situation, and the plans for withdrawal went ahead.

Tripolitania

BP was equally disenchanted with the British foreign policy of accepting a proposal that the mandate for the administration of Tripolitania should be given to Italy:

> I just cannot understand our policy in the Middle East, which seems designed specifically to antagonize Arabs. And what do we get in return? Is HMG prepared for British troops to fight our Arab allies in order to re-instate our ex-enemy Italy in Tripolitania?

He anticipated trouble, and actually ordered a battalion in Cyprus to be ready to move to Tripolitania at short notice. But in the event, it was not needed.

The Final Phase

The end of the Second World War in August 1945 did not bring peace to the Middle East. Indeed, the problems increased, as countries turned their thoughts to the future and their own interests. The 'wind of change' became a 'khamseen' and fanned the flames of nationalism throughout the region – helped by Russian subversion.

At the same time BP found his power to act being increasingly curtailed by requirements to obtain political approval for any military initiatives. He also found himself increasingly at variance, not only with British Government policies in the Middle East, but also with international pressures arising from the growing strength of the 'wind of change'. Being an 'imperialist' at heart, he did not like the loss of power and prestige that he saw happening everywhere in Britain's world; but he was swimming against a strong tide.

Over Palestine, he was unhappy, (as were the Arabs), at the proposals for increased Jewish immigration, together with the removal of restrictions on the sale and transfer of land to Jews:

> It seems almost incredible that the British Government should agree to this, and thus let down the Arabs, and give way to Jewish terrorism. The effect will be serious throughout the Middle East, I fear. (Diary, 25.4.46)

He sought authority to take stronger action against terrorism, but was forbidden to do anything without Cabinet authority.

One bright spot amid the gloom was Greece, which was transferred on 3 February 1946 from the Mediterranean Command to the Middle East. This gave BP the opportunity to visit the country for the first time since the mutinies of 1944, and he gladly took it. He first toured some of the Greek Islands in February 1946, and then on 14 May he visited Athens, where was given a triumphant hero's welcome and invested with the Military Medal of Merit, Class A, the Greek equivalent of the Victoria Cross. He was the first British soldier to be given this award, and it was an honour that he greatly appreciated.

The enthusiastic reception that he received was a heart-warming recognition of his support of the Greek cause and also his sympathetic handling of the mutinies. The occasion was given added significance by the remarkable links between him and his ancestor, General Sir Richard Church (covered further in Chapter 10).

Demobilization

In March 1946 BP went home on leave, and returned on the 26th, accompanied by Winnie, now that wives were allowed in overseas Commands, and they spent the last three months of his tour together in Cairo. Events in the Middle East were now increasingly dominated by political considerations, but there was always the likelihood of trouble militarily. At the same time demobilization had now become a major issue.

BP regarded demobilization as much more than just releasing troops from the Services. He saw it as a great opportunity to give all servicemen the best possible start in civilian life by 'educating' them in the broadest sense of the word; it was, to his mind, a matter of much more than the standard academic programme. It was a question of motivating them to play their part in the running of their country, and to behave as responsible citizens of the great nation to which they belonged. In other words, he wanted to teach them citizenship, and this was to be the start of his next crusade (see Chapter 11).

Way back in October 1944 BP had written:

I talk always about the future, the need for the education of the man in the street, for a revolution in religion, for a higher standard of living in the Army, and for realistic training. I hope I do some good sometimes.

He spoke later to the staff at the General Base Depot at Almaza, where young soldiers were trained on arrival in the Command:

I impressed on them all the opportunity we have of training these lads to be good soldiers and good citizens. (Diary, 6.12.45)

Soon afterwards he wrote:

Went to Early Service at the cathedral. Thought about moral values and why so many things are being done by leaders in the world today for any motive except righteousness, and particularly by the politicians.

In June 1946 came the moment for BP's Farewell Order of the Day, and not surprisingly it followed the same theme:

...Discipline, Comradeship and Faith; and a continued Faith not only in the future of the Army, but also of the British Empire and Commonwealth.... It is these same qualities that we need now in the civil community, as in the Army, to enable us to win the peace, and to justify the sacrifice of those who, for our today, gave their hopes of tomorrow.

He was invited to stay on as C.-in-C. until the end of 1946, but decided that he would like to retire at the end of June, at the same time as Brooke:

Having served under him for close on six years, and been very pleased to do so, I cannot now transfer my loyalty to Monty. (Diary, 2.2.46)

On 8 June he took part in the Victory Parade in London, returning to Cairo in time to welcome Monty on the 11th as the CIGS Designate, and show him round. It was a somewhat depressing picture that he had to paint:

We may have a showdown with the Jews within a week...there may be serious trouble in Tripolitania any day...the Chiefs of Staff think we may have serious trouble in South Persia any day and with no warning...have discussed a plan to send a force to South Persia to protect Abadan and the oil fields...Monty may have simple, decisive, military solutions to these problems, but he will learn otherwise as CIGS! (Diary, 17.6.46)

On 30 June 1946, BP flew back to England, having handed over Middle East Command to General Sir Miles Dempsey.

A very smooth passage. I already feel a sense of relief from responsibility.... I have flown 60,000 miles (nearly 400 flying hours) in 'Rapier' in eleven months.

On 14 October 1946, he retired as the senior General in the British Army, after just forty years' service.

Tributes came in from many directions, and there was high praise in the Press. One letter from a general on his staff gave him particular pleasure:

May I say once more how much I have appreciated serving under you. I always say, and always shall say, that you are the only absolutely honest man I have ever met, and the greatest Englishman I have ever known...

Another member of his staff, who had been closely involved in the Levant crisis, wrote of him:

I have served under many different Chiefs (during the two wars) but I have never met one whom I could serve with such whole-hearted devotion and affectionate admiration as the General. (BP). To me, he represented the very personification of utter integrity, and his subordinates joyfully gave him all they had, because they knew that their efforts, good or bad, would be appraised by him with absolute justice.

As I went among the Syrians after the war, I heard many criticisms about Western policy towards the East during the actual fighting. But when I mentioned the name of General

Paget, I was invariably told 'Ah. General Paget – he, of course, was the great exception – he was an absolutely straight man'.

It was my fortune to be near him during some of the most critical moments of his Middle East Command, and one always had the assurance that the only possible and best possible thing would be done. It was indeed an honour and a delight to serve under him.

Notes
1. On 25 October 1945 he noted, 'C.-in-C.'s Meeting today did not take long, as I was in the Chair.'
2. Nahas Pasha, Prime Minister of Egypt.
3. Note the capital 'T' which he always used for 'the Troops'.
4. Admiral W.G. Tennant, Flag Officer Levant and Eastern Mediterranean.
5. 'Arrangement for the Provision of Security in the Middle East'.

Chapter 10

The Greek Connection

As already mentioned in Chapter 9, when BP took over as C.-in-C. Middle East, the Free Greek Army came under his command, and BP therefore became *ipso facto* Commander-in-Chief of the Greek Army. This was a remarkable instance of history repeating itself, for BP was himself a direct descendant of another British general, Sir Richard Church, who had been C.-in-C. of the Greek Army during the Greek War of Independence (1821-1827). It was a connection of which BP was well aware and also very proud.

Sir Richard Church

Richard Church was born in Cork in 1784, and ran away from home at the age of sixteen. He took the King's Shilling, whereupon his father purchased him a commission in the 13th (Somerset) Regiment in 1800. He fought in the Egyptian Campaign, where he met Greek troops, and felt his first sympathy towards them.

In 1805 he transferred to the 39th Foot (later the Dorset Regiment), and was promptly made Adjutant of the Light Battalion. The decisive moment in his life came four years later, when he was posted to the island of Corfu, recently captured from the French. He spent the next five years there with the task of recruiting and training the local Greeks as soldiers. He showed himself a natural leader of foreign troops, and successfully formed the 1st Regiment of the Duke of York's Greek Light

Infantry; in 1810 he was promoted Major and given command of the Regiment.

The same year he led his men in the capture of the island of Santa Maura, where his left arm was shattered by a bullet (just as happened to BP in 1918!)

His military career continued along unconventional lines, for he next became a Major General in the Neapolitan Army, suppressing brigands (or insurgents as they would now be called) in Apulia 1817-1820.

He did not become involved in the Greek War of Independence until 1826, when Greece was weakening under heavy Turkish pressure. His achievements in Corfu had, however, been remembered and, in 1826, he was formally invited to come to Greece, and take over the Army, in a bid to stave off defeat. On 15 April 1827, he was appointed C.-in-C. of the Greek Army, with Count John Capodistrias as President of Greece, and the British Admiral, Lord Cochrane, as High Admiral of the Greek Navy.

It was a desperate moment in the history of Greece, and within a month, the Army suffered a serious defeat, in an attempt to relieve the siege of Athens. The tide turned however, with the great naval victory of Navarino on 20 October 1827. General Church was then able to take the offensive, which he did by launching a campaign of guerrilla warfare against the Turks in Western Greece. It was successful, and by June 1829, the whole area was liberated. The country was now free at last.

His task completed, General Church promptly resigned as C.-in-C., but he remained in Greece, where he became a highly respected citizen, being appointed Inspector General of the Army in 1836 and a Senator in 1844.

History Does Repeat Itself

General Church was renowned as being outspoken and also a man of great integrity. He was physically tough, riding four miles daily at the age of eighty to swim in the sea. At eighty-seven he was still swimming, but made the concession of driving to the beach in a carriage instead of on horseback. He died in 1873 in his ninetieth year, and was given a national funeral in Athens.

It was said of him 'He fears no one and all the bad men fear him'. This was a tribute that could be applied equally to his great-great-great-nephew, Bernard Paget, and there are other similarities. BP too was a Light Infantry soldier, and he was also, of course, an outstanding trainer of troops of any nation. Indeed, they may both have drawn inspiration from yet another great Light Infantryman, Sir John Moore. There is also the coincidence that they both had disabled left arms.

The final similarity is that one of the problems that faced Richard Church was constant dissension among the Greeks themselves, and BP found the same in 1944. Both of them coped with the problem successfully, and without losing the confidence or the respect of Greece.

Sadly, it did not fall to BP to lead the Greek forces under his command into battle, but in his farewell address to them before they left, his words might have been spoken by Richard Church, 118 years earlier.

> There could be no worse tragedy than that the sufferings of the Greek people should be prolonged by their own disunity. As the British and the Greeks have been united in comradeship in war, so they will remain true comrades in peace.... Do not forget the honour of Greece is in your hands.

A well-known characteristic of Richard Church was his refusal to look after his own interests, particularly in financial matters; he could have made substantial and fully justified claims on the Greek Government for money that he had spent on their behalf, but he never did so. Only when he died was a record found in his papers of what the Government owed him – and he had only compiled that to ensure that he left no debt to others.

A contemporary of Church wrote at the time of his death:

> There has run a solemn seriousness through his life, and a strong sense of duty, reaching far beyond the thought of self-

glory and personal ambition, which distinguishes his life above all his contemporaries.

Every word of this could be said to apply equally to BP, and it is intriguing that characteristics such as these should have emerged again four generations on,[1] together with the remarkable similarities in their careers and achievements.

The Greek Army Mutiny

The position in Greece in April 1944 was that the country had been occupied by the Italians since 1940, and a Greek Government in exile had been set up in Cairo, where the British Ambassador to Greece was Sir Reginald Leeper. The King and Queen of Greece, and also the Crown Prince, were all living in Cairo, and BP had regular contact with them.

The Greek forces that had escaped the occupation were all stationed in the Middle East Command, but there was the complication that Greece as a country was part of the Mediterranean Command under General 'Jumbo' Wilson. 1 Greek Mountain Brigade, stationed in Egypt, and 3 Greek Mountain Brigade in Lebanon were, however, under the command of BP, as was the Greek Navy at Alexandria.

Trouble started on 6 April 1944, when 1 Greek Mountain Brigade mutinied and refused to obey their officers. They were due to go to the fighting in Italy in a week's time, but the cause of the trouble was basically political rather than military, and had been stirred up by Communist agitators. There was also some unrest in the Greek Navy as well as among some merchant ships in Alexandria Harbour; one Captain was thrown overboard by his crew, but the ringleaders were soon arrested, and the situation did not get out of control.

The mutiny in the Army was more serious however, and was a threat to the whole Allied position in the Middle East and also in Italy. It had to be dealt with swiftly, and it was an unwelcome challenge to BP; 'mutiny' was NOT a subject that was normally studied at the Staff College!

Because the issue had so many political implications, BP had to keep in constant and close touch with the politicians on all sides, and to consult them at all times. His first step was to issue orders that the entire brigade was to be disarmed and sent out into the desert, out of the way. He then formally took command of the Greek Army in the Middle East, and banned the Greek Government from having any dealings with the troops. He ordered some tanks to approach the camp, but they were threatened by 17-pounder anti-tank guns, and were told to withdraw, rather than cause bloodshed.

Churchill now became involved and, with his approval, it was decided not to precipitate a confrontation with the mutineers, but to try to negotiate. BP duly opened discussions with them,[2] and was supported by the King of Greece, who made a broadcast. On 11 April BP flew to Alexandria, and met a delegation from the mutineers,[3] but achieved no settlement. 'Much time wasted over these d...... Greek mutineers' he wrote.[4] Fortunately 3 Greek Mountain Brigade in the Lebanon was not affected, and remained loyal.

By 13th the situation seemed to be improving. Two groups of men had escaped from the camp, and some of them agreed to go back and try to persuade others to surrender. On 15th BP had pamphlets dropped from the air, warning that he would soon have to use force, but this did not work. Mr Papandreou arrived in Cairo as a new Greek Prime Minister, and BP was impressed by him. But the situation was growing more serious, with disturbances developing among other Greek troops in Egypt in sympathy with the political aims of the mutineers.

No solution had materialized, and it was agreed that force must be used. On the 21st, BP flew to Alexandria again, and issued orders for a dawn attack on the mutineers' camp on the 24th:

A full day. 0715 to 0130, almost non-stop. (Diary 21.4.44)

On 22nd, boarding parties of loyalist Greeks successfully captured three of the mutinous ships in Alexandria harbour with few casualties, whereupon the others surrendered, and at least the naval mutiny was over.

Then at dawn on 24th, the attack on the 1 Mountain Brigade camp went in as planned. British troops from the British 7

Armoured Brigade broke in and the mutineers laid down their arms; they were then taken to prisoner of war camps 'to be sorted out'. There were no Greek casualties, but one British officer was killed.

The mutiny was now over, and BP received a personal telegram from the PM. 'I congratulate you on the satisfactory reward of your firm and well-considered action.'

He now had a meeting with the King of Greece, and made his proposals for dealing with the aftermath, which looked like being as difficult as the mutiny itself. His proposals were:

a.   All Greek forces to come directly under him as C.-in-C.

b.   An Officers' Selection Board to be set up to screen all officers.

c.   There should be expedited courts martial. 'I did not favour shooting many, but ringleaders should be "sacked" from the Middle East.'

d.   The War Minister to be replaced. (He was arrested next day.)

BP's comment was:

The King agreed to all my proposals and thanked me warmly for my handling of the affair. The Crown Prince did likewise as I left. But I do not think the King has a future.

The problem was not yet completely solved, for unrest continued among Greek units in the Middle East, though on a small scale. BP got on well with Papandreou, who was now Prime Minister, and was proving to be the strong man needed.

...a fine looking man and an optimist; he has done well so far, and has agreed to all my requirements...but he does have some wild ideas.

Sir Reginald Leeper wrote of the affair:

The Greeks were lucky in the two British commanders,

132

General Paget and Admiral Sir John Cunningham, with whom they had to deal.

He could have mentioned that much the same comment might well have been made about the 'two British commanders' in the Greek War of Independence, General Sir Richard Church and Admiral Lord Cochrane.

Reward

Relations with the Greek Army now became normal again and, in August 1944, 1 Greek Mountain Brigade moved to Italy as originally planned. The Brigade Commander Colonel Tsakolotos, wrote to BP:

> This Brigade now has only one ambition – that only good reports may reach you, as a tangible proof of our gratitude and as a repayment to you for all your efforts.
> And when, with God's help, we once more enter GREECE, I assure you, my General, that the whole world will learn that this Brigade is the creation of General Sir Bernard PAGET, a leader, who, like his ancestor, General Church, was a benefactor of our people; and so the Greek people will learn who is the man who wished to re-establish the glory and honour of the Army of Greece.

On 12 October 1944 the Germans pulled out of Greece, and on 17th, Greek troops moved in. It would have been a splendid final touch if BP could have led the Greek Army back into their liberated country, and the Greek Government did indeed ask if this could not be arranged; but sadly it was not to be, because Greece still came under the control of the Mediterranean Theatre.

> I am told that the Greeks are very anxious for me to take command in Greece, and that I should have a very good influence through my relationship to Sir Richard Church; Scobie[5] has also sent me a signal asking me to go to Athens, but I cannot do that unless I am invited by Jumbo Wilson. (Diary. 1.11.44)

Although they had pulled out of Greece, the Germans still remained in occupation of the island of Rhodes until early May. Then, on 15 May, BP joined Archbishop Damaskinos, Regent of Greece, on an official visit to the newly liberated island, and the people duly showed their gratitude.

As BP and the Archbishop drove through streets lined by cheering crowds, they were showered with rose petals and confetti. There were many speeches, and the Regent presented BP with the Grand Cordon of King George I, the highest honour that Greece can bestow. In his speech the Regent declared:

> Your connection with Greece through your great-great-great uncle, Richard Church, makes this event all the more historic. Greece is greatly indebted to you for all you have done for her.

The celebrations culminated in what BP described as 'a huge lunch, which I felt to be very out of keeping with the under-nourished condition of the people of Rhodes'. He showed his feelings by then giving the whole island a week's free rations.

One enthusiastic reporter described the scene:

> Not since the days when the Crusaders rode through the portals of the Castle of St John of Jerusalem has Rhodes seen such carnival, joy, and emotional acclamation.

There were Guards of Honour from the Evzones and the Greek Sacred Regiment, and BP slept that night in the Castle in the suite always reserved for King Victor Emmanuel.

On 5 July 1945 BP addressed the Greek Sacred Regiment on the occasion of their disbandment at the end of the war, in which they had played a gallant role as part of the Greek Raiding Forces.

> You have proved yourselves worthy of your motto 'Victory or Death'. 2000 years ago the first Sacred Regiment established that motto, and died to save Thebes from the Spartans; 120 years ago the second Sacred Regiment did likewise, and preferred death to surrender.
>
> You of the third Sacred Regiment will return to your

homes as victors.... I wish you all good fortune and God Speed.

On 15 March 1946 Greece was, at last, made part of the Middle East Command, and BP now had full and official responsibility for the Greek Army, as had General Sir Richard Church.

Visit to Athens

On 15 May 1946 came the culminating moment in the Greek saga, when BP paid a triumphant, official visit to Athens. First, he addressed the newly-formed Higher Military Council, and was then presented with the Greek Military Medal of Merit, Class A, which is the equivalent of a Victoria Cross, and had never before been awarded to a British officer.

The Greek War Minister laid a wreath on the memorial to Sir Richard Church, and BP and the War Minister then both laid wreaths on the Unknown Warrior's Grave. BP next inspected a parade of Greek troops, and took the salute at a March Past.

The day ended with a splendid ceremony at the Stadium, with an audience of some 100,000 people. BP was expected to make a speech, but the loudspeaker system broke down; then the main feature, a parade of women from all the Greek islands, each in their national costume, was sadly so late that it was almost dark, and the only illumination was the rising moon. But that evening the Acropolis was floodlit in BP's honour, and Sir Richard Church must have looked down with great satisfaction.

The next three days saw BP back to work, visiting units in Athens, before flying with an escort of Greek fighters to Salonika, on to Kavalla, and then back to Athens for a final round of ceremony.

On Sunday 19th, he went to church, and was shown a stained glass window dedicated to Sir Richard Church. During the day there were a series of meetings, and in the evening a conducted tour of the Acropolis.

The next day he visited 13th Division, and commented:

Was much struck by high morale, cheerfulness and useful training, in spite of shortage of officers and experienced

135

NCOs. But amenities were below MEF standards, especially in unit canteens...

On 21st he was back in Rhodes, where he was given the Freedom of the Town of Rhodes, and had one of the main streets named after him, with another being named after Sir Richard Church.

It was the end of a dramatic and heart-warming encounter with Greece, in which the Greek connection with Sir Richard Church was firmly re-established. When he retired, BP happily retained his close links with Greece and, on 21 November 1948, he attended a dinner in London as the guest of the Greek Ambassador, to meet the Queen of the Hellenes:

> Wore the Order of King George I and also the GCB. First time I have done so, and felt very smart. Winston greeted me; v. friendly. He said he was just writing about Norway in his Memoirs, and was v. complimentary about the part I had played. He is likely to be less complimentary later on.... The Queen v. charming, and more understanding of the difficulties I had with the Greeks than she used to be.

Notes
1. BP's mother was Helen Church (1858-1911), who was the grand-daughter of John Church (1781-1828), elder brother of General Sir Richard Church (1784-1873).
2. Churchill to BP, 'I fully concur'.
3. He described the leader of the delegation as 'a nasty piece of work'.
4. 'Quite easy to lose my job over this.'
5. Lieutenant General R. Scobie, GOC Greece.

Chapter 11

Citizenship (1944-1948)

Background

BP had always taken a tremendous interest in education for the Army Forces, and this developed into the wider concept of citizenship, which he saw as a logical and essential step forward from the standard academic curriculum. In his own words, the aim must be 'widespread adult education as an essential of good Citizenship'.

The idea began when he was GOC South Eastern Command in 1941, and accelerated in Home Forces, though it inevitably had to take second place there to training for war, rather than for peace. The importance of citizenship really emerged in the Middle East 1945-1946 when thinking was dominated by the return of servicemen to civilian life, and how they could best be helped to face the challenges of the post-war world.

Amid all the stress and strain of being C.-in-C., first of Home Forces and then in the Middle East, BP fought a crusade from 1940 onwards to tackle what he considered to be the vital problem of education not only for the troops, but also for the youth of the country. He saw education in the Army as one means by which the country could 'win the peace', and he set out his views in his C.-in-C.'s Letter No. 2, which he circulated to all Commanding Officers in the Middle East in May 1945:

We shall be tested more highly in the years ahead than we have been even in war. The evil forces of selfishness, dishonesty, ignorance and apathy will be as difficult to defeat as the Germans and the Japanese...adult education has an immensely important part to play...and we must concern ourselves not only with Education within the Services, but also with linking it up with the needs of the civil community.... It has to make clear how the machinery of Government works and how the affairs of the community, the nation and the Empire are conducted; and it has to develop in us a sense of true citizenship, of personal responsibility, and of mutual obligation, so that we no longer refer to the powers that be as 'they', implying some unknown and remote authority, wholly out of touch with our needs and aspirations, but as 'we', implying an authority we know and understand, and who is quite definitely a member of the team. We shall, in a word, be educated not only to an appreciation of the common benefit to be derived from the State, but of our common obligation to the State, and in particular, of a common responsibility to make democracy work.

Uncompromising and highly relevant words, that apply equally well to our world today – indeed more than ever.

He also saw grave dangers in an unduly dominating Welfare State, in which:

More and more services which were once regarded as the affair of the individual, have now become the responsibility of the State...in many ways the life and well-being of the individual are now largely controlled by national and local administration. This makes the individual accept the benefits without accepting the common obligations which every citizen owes to the State.

These views of 1946 are an intriguing and remarkably far-sighted forecast of what has in fact taken place sixty years on! Never was the State so all-powerful in peacetime, and so interfering, as it is today, and never did what BP called 'the evil forces of selfishness, dishonesty, ignorance and apathy' seem to be so all-powerful. He would be deeply worried by the Britain of 2008!

I cannot at this point resist quoting my favourite extract from

138

a splendid book written by General Glubb Pasha, C.-in-C. of the Jordanian Army during and after the war. It is called *The Fate of Empires*, and is fascinating reading. He quotes, on page 17, the complaints of certain contemporary historians about the moral decline of the people of their country:

> They deeply deplored the degeneracy of the times in which they lived, emphasizing particularly the indifference to religion, the increasing materialism, and the laxity of sexual morals. They lamented also the corruption of the officials of the government, and commented bitterly on the extraordinary influence acquired by popular singers, resulting in a decline in sexual morality...much obscene, sexual language came increasingly into use, such as would not have been tolerated in an earlier age...and there was a marked increase in the influence of women in public life.

No! This is not a description of Britain or any other country in 2008, but was written about Baghdad, the capital of the Arab Empire, in the eighth century AD!

As the end of the war drew near, a pair of doughty warriors emerged, who would together fight for the cause of citizenship. They were BP and the distinguished author, Arthur Bryant; men of similar calibre, who preached the same message.

BP spoke constantly of 'winning the peace':

> If we are to win the peace and establish a better world as a result of this war, we must maintain in peace those qualities which made us great in war, and are the redeeming feature of war. We must learn to put first things first; duty before self-interest, and we must have high moral purpose and belief in ourselves and our Destiny.[1]

He saw education as the key factor in the concept of citizenship:

> Education must not be limited to the mere acquisition of knowledge as the key to social position and wealth.... It is a co-operative venture in search of knowledge and a fuller and more satisfying life, both for the individual and the community.[2]

It was powerful preaching, especially from a soldier, but then BP was the son of a bishop, the nephew of a bishop and the brother of an archbishop.[3] It may also partly explain why he was always know in his Regiment as 'Bish'.

Arthur Bryant too believed strongly in the need for enlightened adult education, and he played his part, not only by writing many fine articles, but also by talking and lecturing to the Armed Forces during the war whenever he could. As he himself put it:

> Over the past four years, as one of a vast army of voluntary lecturers, I addressed audiences ranging from Staff Colleges, Fleet flagships and Army Headquarters to motor torpedo boats and lonely searchlight sites with four men and a dog round a smoking stove – often the most rewarding of all – to places as far apart as the Shetlands and Baghdad.

On 18 March 1945 he wrote in the *Sunday Times*:

> It was perhaps their awareness of the tragic extent to which their victory of 1918 had been thrown away that made the leaders of our Army after Dunkirk such champions of adult education…between them the three Services have achieved in four years the greatest piece of constructive adult education in history…. In such work no consideration of politics has been allowed to obtrude…the approach to every subject is factual, objective and free from partisan presentation.

Would that we could say the same today!

On 9 June 1946 he wrote again, after watching the Victory Parade in London:

> Most important of all, there is a need for a system of education, both at home and at school, which exercises, trains and develops the whole nature of Man – not merely his memory for passing examinations or his brain for doing sums, but his imagination, his perception, his heart, his body, his conscience and his soul; in a word, his whole character…. We stand in need of a great crusade to mobilize

all our talent, all our courage, all our tradition and all our resources...

So it was that the two crusaders came together and fought side by side to promote their vision of a system of national education that would deliberately teach citizenship and thereby make it a major contribution to winning the peace. A great opportunity seemed to appear, when BP retired from the Army in November 1946, and looked for a job where he could 'do something useful'.

In December 1946, he wrote to me:

> I was offered a job by the Military Secretary worth £6,000 a year on the 'Tote', and I told him I would not touch it. Later I was offered a lucrative job in a Brewery, and said the same, not for sanctimonious reasons, but because one owes it to the Army to try and do something worthwhile when one retires as a General, and not something just to make money. I hope that you agree. (Letter, 14.12.46)

Ashridge 1946-1949

Encouraged by Arthur Bryant, BP did however take on the job of Principal of Ashridge College near Berkhamstead in Hertfordshire. It was a magnificent country mansion which had until 1928 been a private house; it was then bought by Mr Urban Broughton, who wanted to make it an educational establishment in memory of his friend, Andrew Bonar Law, who had been the first Canadian-born Prime Minister of Britain.

Broughton accordingly set up a trust to run it as 'a residential college open to all and sundry for the study in short courses of the events and problems of the day and for the encouragement of an informed democracy'. It was named the Bonar Law College, and courses on the lines of the Charter were organized from 1929 to 1939, when it became a wartime Emergency Hospital. It re-opened as a College in 1946, and BP became the first post-war Principal.

He agreed broadly with the principles set out in the Charter, but with one overriding proviso; he was only prepared to take on the job on the strict understanding that it would be completely free of party politics. This raised problems, in that

Ashridge had till now been run by a largely Conservative Governing Body with Conservative Party support, and, since it had the association with Bonar Law, it was generally assumed to be Conservative orientated.

The Governing Body nevertheless agreed to the principle of 'no party politics', as required by BP, and he duly took up his post on 2 December 1946. Lord Davidson, Chairman of the Governing Body, introduced him as the new Principal, describing him as:

> ...Bunyan's Christian gentleman, a gentleman in the best sense.... You will find that he will display those virtues that make a great leader – modesty, humility, an intense dislike of half-truths, a mistrust of all propaganda, and the belief that Truth will ultimately triumph....

BP and Arthur Bryant both saw great possibilities in the work of Ashridge as a means of implementing their ideas for 'winning the peace', and their hopes were high.

BP straight away set out the aims of Ashridge, as he saw them:

> This is a College of Citizenship having for its purpose the education of public opinion through the spread of knowledge and understanding, and the creation of fellowship based on spiritual values, and free from the taint of class or party, nationality or colour. The purpose is of vital importance if we are to redeem the sacrifices of two world wars, and establish a just and lasting peace.

He elaborated this theme in an article in the *Ashridge Journal* in December 1946, and it is worth quoting at some length, because it epitomizes my father's beliefs and hopes:

> How are we to ensure that our time of greatness in war is not forgotten, and that we shall prove worthy in peace of the sacrifices made in two world wars? In fact, having won the war, how are we going to win the peace, which we failed to do after the Kaiser's War? ...I have no doubt myself that the two essentials are religion and education.
>
> To make good the war damage in the rising generation, we

greatly need that type of education which will give to youth an intelligent understanding of the individual's responsibility to make democracy work as an effective agency for the common good; which will give them the right sort of values and standards, by the light of which they can think things out for themselves on sound lines; which will develop in them a sense of true citizenship, of personal responsibility, and of moral obligations, and teach them to appreciate the fact that true freedom derives from discipline and service, and that peace and security are dependent upon the will and the means to defend them. This will be an insurance against apathy, materialism and belief in such ostrich-like slogans as 'safety first'; it will also provide one of the best guarantees we can have for winning the peace and making a better world for men to live in.

Ashridge was formally opened at the end of 1946, and the first course began on 3 January 1947. Arthur Bryant was one of the governors, and he took charge of the educational side alongside BP; they had an enthusiastic, dedicated staff (three strong only), but they all had clear ideas of what they hoped to achieve, as well as high hopes for the future.

The first course lasted four days and was attended by ninety-eight students, aged eighteen to eighty. The subjects covered were all topical and included 'The Individual and the State in the New Age', with Lord Elton as the speaker; 'The Educational System' by Professor Jessop; and 'Past and Future' by Arthur Bryant. With such distinguished lecturers, it should have been a success, and indeed, it was. The students included servicemen, ex-servicemen, business executives and a wide cross-section of society.

By the end of 1947 there had been forty-seven courses involving 3,744 students (compared with 3,476 in 1938). Equally important, the income from fees rose from £10,102 to £12,323.[4] One of the governors, Lord Fairhaven, wrote to BP:

I am extremely pleased with the progress made…. You have done wonders in passing the 1938 figures by such a margin.

Lord Hailsham (also a governor) wrote:

...it seems that you have succeeded in revitalizing the Institute.

The following year, 1948, was equally encouraging, as the reputation of Ashridge spread. BP was adamant that the teaching must remain totally above party politics, and this seemed to be valued by the users of Ashridge. Enrolments went up to 5,400, and the subjects covered were considerably extended, to include matters such as 'Town and Country Planning', 'Society and the Arts', 'Christianity and Education', Industrial Leadership' and 'Training for Industry'.

Students were coming now from almost every sector of the community, which was just what BP and Arthur Bryant wanted; they felt particularly that industry was vitally important.

One of the techniques that BP enjoyed trying out in order to achieve this was to invite some senior figure in a large business concern,[5] preferably the Chairman, to attend a course, and then to arrange for one or more of his subordinates, preferably shop stewards, from the same firm to come on the same course. He would then fix it for them to sit next to each other at dinner – a move which he declared, with some satisfaction, nearly always led to 'much mutual enlightenment'.

But the canker of party politics was beginning to raise its head, and relations with the governing body were showing signs of strain. They were none too happy to hear that Socialists, trade union leaders and even Communists had been attending courses, and taking an active part. BP however, stood firmly by his methods, and made clear that:

...as long as I am Principal, there will be no compromise on the 'no party politics', issue.

On 14 November he ran the largest course yet, 208 strong, with a very impressive list of speakers, and also an encouragingly large number of students from industry.

144

Financial Trouble

But although all was prospering on the educational side, there were serious financial problems looming behind the scenes. Although the income from fees had risen dramatically, so had the costs of running Ashridge, and the College was now facing an annual deficit that was almost half its income.

To date, the College had been subsidized by an annual grant from the Trust, but this source was now running out, and it became evident early in 1949 that it would not be possible to run Ashridge along the present lines beyond the end of that year. The Board decided that the best solution would be to find a permanent source of income rather than the unpredictable income from short courses, and they began looking for some establishment that would meet their needs.

In May 1949 they informed BP that, in view of the uncertain future of Ashridge, he and his educational staff were being given tentative notice that, unless a solution was found, their employment would cease at the end of the year. This unexpected news came as a profound shock and a deep disappointment, particularly when they were doing so well. In the meantime, the courses continued to gain even more support; fifty were organized for 1949, with a total attendance of 5,418, and a record income of £22,000. BP also set about trying to raise £6,000 from industry and other sources.

The Board then came up with their suggested solution to the crisis, which was to arrange for a girls' finishing school in London called the House of Citizenship to move into Ashridge on a permanent basis; it catered for around eighty girls, aged seventeen to twenty-five. BP and Arthur Bryant both disagreed with the proposal, on the grounds that it would mean, in effect, having two Principals at Ashridge, and was not in accordance with BP's terms of reference.

Nevertheless, on 8 September the Board decided that they would accept the House of Citizenship as part of Ashridge.[6] They also confirmed the dismissal of BP and his staff at the end of the year.

BP considered that, in the circumstances, his position at Ashridge was now untenable, and he offered to leave earlier than the end of the year. This was accepted by the Board, and he and his staff were told to leave by 11 October, which they did, and Arthur Bryant resigned as a governor at the same time.

This wrecking of their hopes and plans was a bitter disappointment to both BP and Arthur Bryant, the more so because of the manner of it. There was comfort however in the flood of letters expressing protest, sympathy and appreciation that poured in from both lecturers and students. This support was also expressed in the Press, and a bitter public row developed,[7] which was something that BP found most unwelcome and unpleasant. He disliked it intensely, but was not one to back away from a fight for a just cause and, much though he resented having to do it, he fought fiercely for his crusade.

It was, however, to no avail, and on 11 October he moved out of Ashridge with sadness and some bitterness. But good was to come out of ill, for he was now offered the job of Governor of the Royal Hospital, Chelsea.

Notes
1. Talk to Shrewsbury School, 1943.
2. 'C.-in-C.'s Letter Number 1' in the Middle East.
3. Francis, Bishop of Oxford (1901-1911), Luke, Bishop of Chester (1919-1932), Edward, Bishop of Southern Rhodesia (1925-1955), Archbishop of Central Africa (1955-1957).
4. A weekend course cost three guineas.
5. Firms now sending students included BOAC, Vickers Armstrong, Marks and Spencer, Cadbury, four major banks, Tate and Lyle and Distillers.
6. From 1953 a new life began for Ashridge, when, by an Act of Parliament, it was allowed to qualify as an official charity. This greatly improved the financial position and it was able to continue as a centre for adult education, as originally envisaged by its founder.
7. One headline read 'Debs Oust Famous General!'

Chapter 12

The Royal Hospital (1949-1957)

Our new home at the Royal Hospital promises to be a happy one, and anyway, it is a great relief to be back in the Army

BP moved into the Royal Hospital as Governor in November 1949, and was delighted to be back with soldiers and a way of life that he knew and loved. Everything about the appointment appealed to him, and seven happy years lay ahead. He always enjoyed any occasion of history and tradition, be it a service in Westminster Abbey, the Queen's Birthday Parade or a Presentation of Colours.

Now, everything at the Royal Hospital was just what he appreciated; the beauty of the Wren buildings, the Sunday Church Parades, and the annual celebrations of Founder's Day. Above all, there were the Pensioners themselves, proud old soldiers of many Regiments, who had served Queen and Country round the world, and he greatly looked forward to the chance to look after them.

The Royal Hospital was founded in 1682 by King Charles II to provide a home for retired soldiers of the Standing Army, which had been established twenty-one years earlier. It was not completed until 1692, to a design by Sir Christopher Wren, and today it offers a happy home to some 300 Chelsea Pensioners, well known in their scarlet coats and tricorne hats. The qualifications for becoming an In-Pensioner are that anyone applying to join must be in possession of an Army Pension, have an official 'Good Character', be over sixty-five, and must also be 'without encumbrance', which means having no wife.

This last requirement led to one Pensioner, aged eighty-four, marching in to the Governor to ask for permission to leave the Royal Hospital. BP was worried that he must be unhappy about something at Chelsea, and asked him what the problem was. 'No problem, Sir. It's just that I want to get married.' Relieved, but curious, BP asked him how old his fiancée was: 'Oh, she's only eighty-one, Sir,' came the reply.

The average age of 'recruits', as new arrivals are called, is currently about eighty-two and there are usually several pensioners aged over 100, some of whom still appear on parade on Founder's Day. They have to give up their pension on arrival, and are then fed, clothed and housed, and are also entitled to a pint of bitter a day, as decreed by King Charles II.

The Governor is a retired Field Marshal or full General, and there is also a Lieutenant Governor, who is a Major General. The staff under them consists of an Adjutant, a Quartermaster, a Medical Officer and a Chaplain, who between them run the day-to-day business of the Hospital. There are also four Captains of Invalids, who are retired Army officers, each nominally in command of a 'company' of Pensioners.

As always, BP soon set about seeing what could be improved, and in particular, he did much for the welfare of the Pensioners. He began by getting their cubicles (or 'bunks') enlarged from the 6 foot by 6 foot designed by Wren, which was so small that a man had to step out into the passage to put on his trousers! By 1956 he had got this changed to 9 foot by 6 foot, which made all the difference, and added greatly to the comfort of every Pensioner.[1]

Another major change was the introduction of central messing. This had been Wren's original intention, but for the last 150 years the Pensioners had been fed in their 'bunks'; this meant that the food was not always hot, and also that it was not feasible to give them an evening meal.

BP called this arrangement 'messy and insanitary', and, having first re-equipped and reorganized the kitchens, he established the magnificent Great Hall[2] as a central dining room. As a result the Pensioners fed together, had a greater variety of meals (that were always hot), were waited on, and also received supper. The new dining room was formally opened on

Founder's Day 1955, and was welcomed by everyone. A month later, BP was able to comment:

The only danger at present is that the old men will eat too much!

The many changes that BP was always demanding all required the sanction of the War Office and also the Ministry of Works, as well as meetings with the Board of Commissioners of the Royal Hospital to discuss the financial implications. There was also the perpetual problem that any innovation had to conform to the Statutes laid down by King Charles II! As a result, it was a slow process, and BP once complained that:

If the mills of God grind slowly, they are jet-propelled compared with the mills of the Royal Hospital!

So it came to pass that BP wrote to the War Office one day:

In accordance with the instructions laid down by our Founder, I believe I am entitled, as Governor, to a carriage and pair to convey me on the duties of the Hospital to Whitehall and elsewhere. Could you therefore please arrange for my carriage to be available next Wednesday at 11 o'clock to convey me to Whitehall?

Happily, the letter arrived on the desk of someone at the War Office, who also had a sense of humour, and he duly received the reply:

Dear General,

Thank you for your request for a carriage and pair next Wednesday. Alas, one of the horses is lame, and one of the wheels of the carriage has lost several spokes in an accident, and is unserviceable.
    Would you settle for an Austin Princess?

BP accepted, adding 'Fifteen All!'

On 24 May 1951 BP attended a Service of the Order of the Bath in Westminster Abbey, and wrote in his diary:

It is my hope that I may live long enough to be installed, and to hang my Banner in Henry VII's Chapel.

Happily, he did, and that proud moment came on 27 October 1960, just a year before he died.

He also recorded:

One of the Colour Sergeants told me today that I was still a fighting General, and had done more for the Royal Hospital in my time than had been done in the previous 300 years! I am glad to be appreciated by these old soldiers – but glad also that my predecessors did not hear what the Colour Sergeant said!

But a less complimentary comment came from a Labour MP in the House of Commons, who, during a debate on the Army Estimates on 10 March 1952, claimed that the Royal Hospital was run by 'martinets with military minds'. Fortunately, a Conservative MP present had been on BP's staff during the war as a Brigadier, and he promptly retorted:

The officer who is at present in charge of the Hospital has a record second to none in the British Army for the deep concern that he has shown in practical form for the true welfare of the soldier, when he is serving and when he is retired.

A very important part of the hospital is the In-Pensioners Club, where the Pensioners can gather for a drink, chat, play bowls and also entertain their friends. BP felt that improvements could and should be made, and he spent a comparatively large sum on refurnishing and decorating the Club, an initiative that was much appreciated.

The Chapel is very much a feature at the Royal Hospital, and attendance at Church is a traditional part of life there, with the Governor, Lieutenant Governor or Adjutant always attending to read the Lesson. BP used to give all the preachers a stern warning that 'sermons are not to last more than seven minutes; that is long enough for the old men'. The Governor's pew faced the pulpit, and on the dot of the seventh minute, if the preacher was still holding forth, BP would ostentatiously pull out a large fob watch from his breast pocket, hold it up in full view of the preacher, stare at it hard, and then replace it. This would be repeated every minute thereafter until the preacher stopped! BP maintained that no sermon in his time ever lasted over ten minutes!

One occasion when this rule was NOT enforced was on 20 July 1952, when his brother, Edward, preached, when he was Bishop of Southern Rhodesia. He was later to become the first Archbishop of Central Africa, and it was a very happy occasion for them to be together.

Another happy family occasion came when Diana Farmer and I were married in the Chapel on 3 December 1954, and had a wedding reception afterwards in the Council Chamber.

BP had from the start wanted to make a personal gift to the Chapel, and he chose to present a silver gilt Cross to match the 1687 silver gilt Communion Plate of King James II. The Cross was duly made, and was dedicated in the Chapel by the Bishop of London on 21 March 1954, inscribed with the words:

> To the Glory of God and in memory of all Soldiers who have given their lives in the Service of their Country, and of all members of the Royal Hospital who have passed to their rest.

The medical care of so many old men is clearly all-important, and there has always been an infirmary in the grounds of the Hospital; it is a great comfort, and a very proper principle, that the Pensioners know that, if they are bed-ridden, they can still remain in familiar surroundings and among their comrades.

The original infirmary was unfortunately destroyed by a landmine in 1941,[3] and a new, up-to-date one was built and opened in 1960. BP naturally took a keen interest in this during his time, and it contains a 'Paget Ward'.

Farewell

BP's five-year term as Governor was due to end in 1954, but to his great delight, he was twice offered an extension of a year, which he gladly accepted. But finally in 1957 came the sad moment when he had to leave. That year saw the usual series of events at the Royal Hospital, such as the Christmas Carol Service, concerts by military bands, the Chelsea Flower Show, and of course, Founder's Day but this time, they were:

> ...occasions tinged with sadness for Winnie and me, because they are the last for us at the Royal Hospital.

BP's last Founder's Day Parade was inspected by Field Marshal Lord Alexander of Tunis, an old comrade in arms, which was a great pleasure for him. Then, on 22 September, his first grandchild, Olivia, was christened in the Chapel in the new font that had been presented by BP and designed by his cousin, Paul Paget, Surveyor to the Fabric of St Paul's.

On 12 October the staff of the Hospital gave a farewell party for the Governor and his wife in the Great Hall, with all the Pensioners present:

> Such a thing had never been done before, and we were very touched by the genuine affection and loyalty which inspired the occasion.

They were both also made Life Members of the Pensioners' Club, a great and unique honour.

On 22 November 1955 BP stirred the plum pudding for the last time at the traditional 'Pudding Ceremony', and on 27th he enjoyed a memorable dinner in the Council Chamber, attended by the Queen. It was given by the Army Council, and was, as BP said, 'a grand finale for me'.

On 29th he drove away from the Royal Hospital after perhaps the happiest seven years of his life. As he and his wife left, the staff and Pensioners lined the road – another spontaneous and unprecedented tribute.

Notes
1. They have since been enlarged yet again to 9 foot by 9 foot.
2. Every Battle Honour of the British Army since 1662 is listed on panels on the walls of the Great Hall – the only place with the complete record on display.
3. It was on the site of the present National Army Museum. Now, in 2008, yet another infirmary is being built on the site of the present building, which adjoins the hospital.

Chapter 13

Retirement (1956-1961)

When BP left the Royal Hospital at the end of 1956, he went to live at the Old Orchard in Petersfield, Hampshire; it was the first permanent home he had ever had in his life, and, except for two and a half years at Oxford from 1930, the only house he had ever owned.

Not surprisingly, he never for a moment considered sitting back and relaxing, but promptly undertook even more voluntary work, directing his efforts at the young and the old, the needy, and above all, the ex-servicemen and women.

As long as I am able to do so, I feel it a definite duty to work for the disabled of two world wars and for their dependents.

The list of the main appointments he held demonstrates his interests:

Colonel, The Oxfordshire and Buckinghamshire Light Infantry (43rd and 52nd).

Colonel of the Intelligence Corps.

Colonel of the Reconnaissance Regiment.

Governor of four schools (Radley, Eastbourne, St Edwards and Welbeck).

President of the Army Benevolent Fund.

Chairman of the Royal Cambridge Home.

Vice President of the Royal Commonwealth Society for the Blind.

Vice Chairman of the Disabled Ex-Servicemen's Exhibition.

Chairman of the Appeals Branch of the Forces Help Society.

Chairman of a King George's Jubilee Trust Working Party.

Council of the Officer's Association.

Embankment Fellowship Society.

Council of the National Rifle Association.

Trustee of the Staff College Museum.

Life Governor, the Corps of Commissionaires.

Vice President, Church Lads Brigade.

In 1960 he was appointed a Deputy Lieutenant of Hampshire, which he much appreciated.

He received a War Gratuity of £387, and commented that 'it is not much compared to what Haig and Co got, but I do not think Regular soldiers should receive any gratuity'.

The Regiment

BP always maintained the closest possible touch with his Regiment, particularly after his retirement in 1946, and in October of that year he became its Colonel, a position that he held with the greatest pride for the next nine years.

In 1948 he had to agree to the amalgamation of the 43rd and the 52nd; though he realized it was an inevitable decision, it was not one he accepted easily. Henceforth there was only one battalion of his Regiment, the 1st Battalion Oxfordshire and Buckinghamshire Light Infantry (43rd and 52nd).[1]

He carried out his duties as Colonel of the Regiment with his usual thoroughness, and his work is perhaps best summed up by an extract from the *Regimental Chronicle*:

Soon after he assumed the Colonelcy, General Paget, to the lasting benefit of the Regiment in general, took over the Chairmanship of the Regimental Committee, and hardly missed one meeting in the course of his nine years tenure of office.

In fact he was constantly at Cowley Barracks, driving himself backwards and forwards to London in all weathers and at all times of the year, taking the passing-out parades of the recruits, attending Old Comrades reunions and being present at most of the parties in the Officers Mess; in fact, all the major activities of life at Regimental Headquarters. His visits to the Battalion abroad were numerous and greatly appreciated.

His period as Colonel of the Regiment coincided with a great bout of Regimental ceremonial.

In 1950 there was a Service of Dedication of the Roll of Honour for the Second World War, and the unveiling of the Regimental Memorial Tablet in the Regimental Chapel in Christ Church Cathedral, Oxford. BP had himself initiated the establishment of this Chapel in 1930, and so this was a particularly satisfying occasion for him.

In November 1952 he flew out to the Middle East to visit the Regiment, and was lent the personal plane of the C.-in-C. Transport Command, which he much appreciated.

In 1953 came the celebration of the 150th anniversary of the formation of the Light Brigade at Shorncliffe, and in May 1954 BP presented new Colours, on behalf of the Queen, to the 1st Battalion (43rd and 52nd) in Osnabruck. He thoroughly enjoyed the day, and wrote:

A great occasion. Drill, turnout and steadiness on parade were flawless. The Service of Dedication was very impressive.

BP's final parade as Colonel of the Regiment was held at Osnabruck on 14 October 1955 to celebrate the bicentenary of the 52nd Light Infantry. He took the Salute, in the company of his successor, Major General Sir John Winterton, and wrote:

The turn-out, steadiness and drill were faultless. The old 52nd Colours were trooped for the last time, but, as they disappeared off parade, Reveille was sounded in token of the continued existence of the 52nd...at the end I addressed the Battalion, this being my last parade as Colonel of the Regiment, and it could not have been more perfect and impressive.

The next day I had a wonderful and moving send-off, which was almost too much for me. Sergeants formed a Guard of Honour on the stairs leading up to the platform and Buglers sounded fanfares. There was a large crowd to see us off.

His record as Colonel was appropriately summed up in the *Regimental Chronicle*:

It would be an under-statement to say that no Colonel of the Regiment has ever done more than General Paget to further the interests of the Regiment. He has been likened to another great Colonel of the Regiment – General Sir John Moore. Certainly, he seemed to wear his mantle during his Colonelcy, and he indeed inspired the young and fortified the old. He was also the most approachable Colonel that can ever have been.

A rather less impressed comment on his Colonelcy came from the War Office in the shape of an official letter (signed, rather strangely BP thought, by the Director of Finance!) expressing 'the sincere thanks of the Army Command for the valuable services rendered to the Regiment during your tenure of appointment as Colonel'. BP's comment was:

This is better than the letter I received on retiring in July 1946, having been a...C.-in-C. for four and a half years. Then the thanks were not even 'sincere', and the signature was printed!

A rather more sincere tribute came from a friend who described him as 'the greatest infantry soldier ever'.

Last Years

In 1958 BP accepted the Chairmanship of the Forces Help Society, but with some reluctance, saying:

I think I now have as much as I can tackle with reasonable efficiency.

This work meant much travelling, with long periods of standing, which aggravated the worsening pain in his arthritic joints. But he carried on, and wrote to Arthur Bryant:

My attitude in life has always been to look at the bow wave, and not look back at the wake. And though my bow wave is now a very small one, I hope, and believe, it is still there.

His old school, Shrewsbury, was eager to pay tribute to one of their most distinguished Old Boys, and in 1959 the Governors commissioned a portrait of him to be painted by William Dring, RA. It was exhibited in the Royal Academy in 1960, and now hangs in the School.

On 27 October 1960 came a moment that BP had long wanted and waited for, his installation as a Knight Grand Cross of the Order of the Bath. He proudly took part in the service in Westminster Abbey, and saw his Banner hung in the Henry VII Chapel.

He wrote of his Banner:

It displays the Paget coat of arms*, and I chose as my Supporters a Greek Evzone in full dress, as a link with Sir Richard Church, the Greek Sacred Regiment, and the 3rd Mountain Brigade of Rimini fame; also a Crusader; with the badge of Home Forces on his shield and the red cross of 21st Army Group on his tunic.

It was in fact only just in time, for he died of a heart attack on 16 February 1961, aged seventy-four.

A Memorial Service was held in the Chapel of the Royal Hospital, Chelsea on 24 February 1961. Representatives of The

* See page xiii.

Queen, The Duke of Gloucester and The Princess Royal were present, as were three Field Marshals (Alanbrooke, Festing and Templer) and thirty-three Generals. Field Marshal Montgomery sent his regrets at being unable to attend.

There were many tributes from many people, not only Field Marshals and statesmen, but private soldiers, drivers, Greeks and Poles, men and women from all walks of life who had known and admired him, and BP would have appreciated their sincere words most of all.

One tribute of particular interest came from the German general, Baron Geyr von Schweppenburg, who had been German Military Attaché in London in the 1930s, and had worked with BP who was then in the War Office to try to stop the war starting (see Chapter 3). He ended the war commanding a Panzer Army in France in 1944, and survived.

He now wrote to BP's widow:

I, during my service period in your country did not meet two more chivalrous and admirable soldiers than Sir John Dill and Sir Bernard Paget. What missing means to the human heart, I presently feel it myself. Sir Bernard, brilliant and dedicated soldier that he was, reached the highest ethical standards in his profession, working for peace. In this world he got no credit for his noble endeavour.

BP's achievements in life can perhaps be best summed up by two of his best friends.

The first is an extract from *Prejudice and Judgment*[2] by The Rt. Hon Sir James Grigg, who was Secretary of State from 1942 to 1945:

It was on his creation of what was possibly the finest British Army of all time that I base the assertion that Paget rendered matchless service to the state.

Mr Churchill once referred to Montgomery as 'that great Cromwellian soldier'. I thought then and I think now that the epithet applied much more fittingly to Paget. He was serious – though not at all glum; ascetic, brave, pious; he combined a firm sense of discipline with a deep desire for the welfare of every man under his command, and he insisted on the responsibility of officers not only for the efficiency of their soldiers, but for their material and moral well-being. Above all, he was determined that the whole force should be possessed by his own burning conviction of mission.

Another true friend was Sir Arthur Bryant, and he wrote a tribute to him in 1960:[3]

The nobility and selflessness of the man were apparent to everyone who worked with him. By many of those who knew him, he will be remembered as the supreme embodiment of what a British soldier should be – a man of rocklike character, high moral and physical courage, unfaltering in obedience and in the performance of his duty, yet always eager to encourage initiative in others.

Throughout his career he has been guided, like Havelock and Gordon, by a deep, religious faith and a crusader's sense of mission. Such men arouse love and loyalty in those who serve under them, and leave behind an abiding impress.

Notes
1. In 1957 the title was changed to 1st Battalion, The Royal Green Jackets (43rd and 52nd). Then in 2007 it was changed yet again when the Regiment bacame part of The Rifles.
2. *Prejudice and Judgment*, (page 366).
3. *The Salopian*, June 1960.

Chapter 14

The Crusader

There was a Knight, a most distinguished man,
Who from the day on which he first began
To ride abroad, had followed chivalry
Truth, honour, greatness of heart, and courtesy.

(Prologue to *The Canterbury Tales*, Chaucer)

The portrait that emerges from this story so far is of great achievement by a dedicated soldier, and I would like now to portray something more of my father as a person, rather than as a C.-in-C.

He always knew that he wanted to be a soldier, and that strengthened his sense of purpose. He certainly possessed the traditional qualities – courage, both physical and mental; drive and determination in all he did; robustness, that quality so highly prized by Field Marshal Wavell; a fine brain and a remarkable capacity for hard work. He believed totally in Service before Self, and expected others to have the same belief. Fame and fortune meant nothing to him, but achievement and integrity meant all.

For him the overriding criterion in life was honour and duty. General Horrocks, himself a fine example of these virtues, wrote of him that he was 'one of the most honourable men I have ever met',[1] while another general who served under him described him as 'the only absolutely honest man I have ever met'.[2]

He was essentially a very simple person, who enjoyed the simple things of life, well summed up in a diary note in 1936, in which he listed what gave him most pleasure:

My sons and their progress; early morning and the dew; the BBC's Epilogue; the colours and freshness of Spring; a good fish on the dry fly; completion of a difficult task; an unexpected kindness.

He was also a remarkably modest man (a quality not found in all commanders). He never sought publicity or personal glory, nor did he seek to justify himself in public – hence his refusal to write any memoirs after the war.

Outwardly, he might be considered by those who did not know him well to be somewhat austere and stern, but he was, in fact, extremely human and approachable, particularly where his subordinates were concerned. He had a very lively sense of humour and a ready twinkle in his eye, together with a strong dislike of pomposity or vanity in any form.

Intriguingly, he was described by some as having the qualities of a Cavalier, while others saw him as more like a Roundhead! To my mind, he had some of the better qualities of each, and I personally saw him above all as a Crusader.

Certain events in his life had a definite influence on his attitudes. His ecclesiastical upbringing at Christ Church and Cuddesdon, together with the examples set by his parents, certainly led to his own high principles, and his belief in the importance of religion in life. This background undoubtedly inspired the strong sense of service and duty that dominated his every action.

The First World War, with its terrible loss of life, made a deep and lasting impression on him, and left him with a conviction that 'never again' must such a slaughter be allowed to happen. Hence his crusade in the Second World War to develop Battle Drill, not only as a vital part of training, but also as a means of reducing casualties.

His experiences in the First World War also led him to develop a profound admiration and affection for the British soldier, who was to him 'someone for whom we, as Commanders and on the Staff, can never do too much'. He understood the men and had a remarkable rapport with them; it was a relationship that led to mutual respect, and to an exceptional loyalty from those under him, at all levels. He wrote that:

...the sense of comradeship between Officers and Other Ranks is to my mind the redeeming feature of war, and the finest thing in the Army.

He truly saw the Second World War as a crusade against the forces of evil, and he constantly referred to it as such. He even exhorted his padres to play their part!

Surely this is a Crusade for the establishment of Right against Might; Your main purpose is to establish the crusading spirit, and to strengthen our fighting efficiency through the maintenance of high morale....

He had no hesitation in setting out his beliefs, not only in talks to the Army, but also to civilians, young and old. Hence, when he addressed a group of hard-bitten editors from the Press, whom he had invited to visit to GHQ Battle School to see the work being done there, he took the opportunity to spread his gospel of 'crusading'. It worked, and was reflected in their articles afterwards. (see page 84)

His message was simple and uncompromising:

We cannot hope to win this war outright unless...we make of it a crusade to preserve the liberties of mankind and millions of our fellows.... Let us now wage total war not defensively for possessions, but offensively against evil; not just to preserve our island home, but for the ideals of tolerance, fair play, freedom of thought and speech, kindliness, and the value of the human soul.

We need now to inspire the people with the crusading spirit, and with those ideals for which men will be willing to sacrifice themselves.

But that was only the first stage. Having won the war, we had to win the peace. Like most senior military commanders, he did all he could to look after the interests of all ex-servicemen after the war. He set out to ensure not only that they were properly treated and respected, but also that they were given a proper education so that they would have the best possible opportunities in civilian life.

Linked with that was his concern for the future of the whole nation. He felt that the qualities that had won the war were being replaced by self-interest, a lowering of moral standards and a decline in religion. Hence his post-war crusade aimed at promoting citizenship for the benefit of the whole nation.

This attempt to paint a portrait of my father is perhaps best summed up in his own words in an address that he gave to the cadets at Sandhurst on the occasion of their Passing Out Parade on 29 July 1943:

> It is not by chance that General Alexander's 18th Army Group, the First Army, the Eighth Army and my 21st Army Group all carry a Crusader's Cross as their sign. We adopted that sign because we believe that we are fighting a Crusade against the powers of darkness, and that the Almighty is on our side.
>
> And when the war is won, we must carry the same crusading spirit and the same belief into the task of winning the peace. For it is not material wealth, nor ease and comfort, which will make a better world for all men, but high moral purpose and faith in our Destiny. So do not be shy of declaring your faith....

Surely that is the faith of a true Crusading General.

Notes
1. *A Full Life*, Philip Warner, page 74.
2. Letter, 27.5.46.

Appendix A

The Life of Bernard Paget

Date	Event
15.9.1887	Born at Christ Church, Oxford
1901	Moved to Cuddesdon
1901-1906	At Shrewsbury School
1906	To Royal Military Academy, Sandhurst
13.11.07	Commissioned into Oxfordshire Light Infantry (43rd and 52nd)
15.12.07	Joined 2nd Bn (52nd) at Tidworth
5.2.08	Transferred to 1st Bn (43rd) at Lucknow
2.9.11	Father died
1912-1914	At School of Musketry at Satara
30.8.14	Adjutant, 5th Bn at Aldershot
20.5.15	Bn moved to France
10.6.15	Promoted Captain
17.10.15	Immediate award of MC
29.11.15	Brigade Major, 42 Brigade
12.3.17	Awarded Italian Silver Medal for Valour
3.6.17	Promoted Brevet Major
2.9.17	GSO 2, 62nd Division
27.12.17	GSO 2, GHQ BEF
1.1.18	Awarded DSO
26.3.18	Wounded and evacuated to UK
2.2.18	Married Winnie Paget
24.9.18	GSO 2 at Senior Staff School in Cambridgeshire
8.2.19	GSO 2 (Ops), GHQ BEF

17.3.19	Brigade Major, Aldershot
11.8.19	GSO 2, Aldershot Command
22.1.20	Student at the Staff College, Camberley
1.3.21	GSO 2, War Office (MI 3)
1925-1926	Company Commander, 1st Bn (43rd) in Cologne
1.7.25	Promoted Brevet Lieutenant Colonel
22.1.25	Directing Staff at the Staff College, Camberley
14.1.29	Student at Imperial Defence College
1.7.29	Promoted Colonel
15.2.30	Commanded Regimental Depot at Oxford
1.4.32	Directing Staff at Staff College in Quetta
21.7.34	GSO 1, War Office (MI 3)
1937-1938	Commander 4th (Quetta) Infantry Brigade
29.12.37	Promoted Major General
1938-1939	Commandant at Staff College, Camberley
30.11.39	GOC 18th Division in Norwich
20.4.40	Commands SICKLE FORCE at Andalsnes in Norway
5.6.40	Appointed Acting Lieutenant General. Appointed CB
5.5.40	Chief of Staff to C.-in-C. Home Forces
15.2.41	GOC.-in-C. South Eastern Command
5.8.41	Promoted Lieutenant General
24.12.41	C.-in-C. Home Forces. Appointed KCB
13.7.43	C.-in-C. 21st Army Group. (to 24.12.43)
6.1.44	C.-in-C. Middle East. Appointed GCB. Appointed ADC to the King
4.3.43	Son, Tony, awarded Immediate DSO, but later died of wounds
14.10.46	Retired at own request
Oct 46-Sep 55	Colonel of The Regiment, Oxfordshire and Buckinghamshire Light Infantry (43rd and 52nd)

1946-1949	Principal, Ashridge College of Citizenship
1949-1956	Governor of The Royal Hospital, Chelsea
1957-1961	Retired to Petersfield
27.10.60	Installed as GCB
16.2.61	Died, aged seventy-four

Appendix B

Original Sources

Diaries

BP kept a personal diary most of his life and particularly during the Second World War. He wrote it day-by-day in his own hand, as an account of the day's work, people met, decisions made, frustrations and successes. The diaries have not been published and, in accordance with my father's wishes, will not be. I have quoted selective extracts, but have tried to avoid criticism or controversy.

Talks

BP gave many talks and addresses on military matters and citizenship.

Correspondence

There are many personal letters written by BP, and also to him, including many famous and interesting figures, such as Sir James Grigg, Field Marshals Smuts, Alanbrooke, Dill and Montgomery.

Paget Family History

BP's brother, Humphrey wrote an excellent family history, covering four generations.

SKYSCRAPER

BP kept a copy of the plan, and also his correspondence about it after the war.

Selected Bibliography

Alanbrooke, Lord, *War Diaries, 1939-1945*, Weidenfeld & Nicolson, 2001

Barnett, Corelli, *Britain and her Army*, Allen Lane, 1970

Bryant, Arthur, *Triumph in the West*, Collins, 1959

Buckley, Christopher, *Norway. The Commandos. Dieppe*, HMSO, 1951

Collier, Basil, *The Defence of the UK*, HMSO, 1957

Corrigan, Gordon, *Blood, Sweat and Arrogance*, Weidenfeld & Nicolson, 2006

De Guingand, François, *Operation Victory*, Hodder & Stoughton, 1947

Derry, Dr T.K., *Official History of the Norway Campaign*, HMSO, 1952

Eisenhower, Dwight D., *Crusade in Europe*, Heinemann, 1948

Ellis, L.F., *Victory in the West*, HMSO, 1993

Fergusson, Bernard, *The Watery Maze: the story of Combined Operations*, Collins, 1961

Fraser, David, *And We Shall Shock Them*, Hodder & Stoughton, 1983

Geyr von Schweppenburg, Leo, *The Critical Years*, Alan Wingate, 1952

Glover, William, *Invasion Scare, 1940*, Leo Cooper, 1990

Hamilton, Nigel, *Monty*, Hodder & Stoughton, 1981

Harvey, Maurice, *Scandinavian Misadventure*, Spellmount, 1990

Hay, Ian, *Arms and the Men*, Collins, 1951

Kersaudy, François, Norway 1940, Collins, 1990

Livingstone, Sir Richard, *The Future in Education*, Cambridge University Press, 1945

— *Education for a World Adrift*, Cambridge University Press, 1943

Montgomery, Field Marshal B.L., *Normandy to the Baltic*, BAOR, 1946

— *Memoirs*, Collins, 1958

Morgan, F.E., *Overture to Overlord*, Hodder & Stoughton, 1950

Moulton, J.L., *The Norwegian Campaign of 1940*, Eyre & Spottiswoode, 1966

North, John, *North West Europe, 1944-45*, HMSO, 1977

Ruge, Otto, *History of the Great War – (Norway, 1940)*, Halvorsen & Laursen, 1946

Thompson, R.W., *The Price of Victory*, Constable, 1960

Wigram, Lionel, *Battle Drill and the British Army*, np or d

Wilmot, Chester, *The Struggle for Europe*, Collins, 1952

Index

1st Greek Mountain Brigade, 105, 130-3

1st Green Howards, 30, 36, 38, 40

1st KOYLI, 30, 32, 33, 34, 38

1st Leicestershire Regiment, 30

3rd Greek Mountain Brigade, 130-1

21st Army Group, vii, 51, 56, 67, 68, 77-93, 94-100, 101, 158

airborne troops, 61, 71, 74

air support, 32, 34-6, 38, 42, 49, 80

Ajax, 49-50

Alanbrooke, Field Marshal Lord, x, 45-7, 49, 54-6, 72, 95-100, 106, 124

Aldershot, 6, 7, 11, 165-6

Alexander, Field Marshal Lord, 56, 96, 98, 152

Andalsnes, 26-43

Arras, 9, 10

Ashridge College, 139-46, 166

Athens, 135

Bailey, Lieutenant Colonel V.T., 13

Barclay's Bank, 89-91

Barnard Castle, 83, 84

Battle Drill, 10, 15, 49, 53, 77-93, 162

Battle School, 78-93

Beichmann, Lieutenant Colonel, 30

Berney-Ficklin, Brigadier H.P.M., 29

Bevin, Ernest, 118

Beynet, General, 113-15

Bradley, General Omar, 56

Braithwaite, Major General W., 11, 109

Brigades:
  7 Armoured, 131-2
  15 Infantry, 30-2
  42 Infantry, 7-9, 39, 43n
  148 Infantry, 30-2, 43n

Brooke-Popham, Air Chief Marshal Sir Robert, 50

Bryant, Arthur, 26, 91-2, 108-9, 139-46, 161, 170

Caen, 61, 66

Cambridge, 12
Capodistrias, John, 128
Carton, Lieutenant General
   A., 28
Casablanca, 62
Chamberlain, Neville, 41
Cherbourg, 60, 61
Chester, 7n
Chiefs of Staff, 50, 52, 58, 59,
   62
Christ Church, Oxford, 1-4,
   7n, 16, 156, 162, 165
Church, Helen, 2, 136
Church, John, 2, 136
Church, Mary, 2, 3, 4
Church, Richard, General Sir,
   105, 123, 127-36, 158
Church, Richard, The
   Reverend, 2
Churchill, Winston, 49-50, 51,
   54, 56-8, 83-4, 96, 97, 105,
   106, 113-15, 136, 159
Churchill tank, 54
citizenship, vii, 124, 137-46,
   163, 164, 166
Citizenship, House of, 145
Cochrane, Admiral Lord, 128,
   133
COSSAC, 62, 64, 67, 68, 69, 98
Cologne, 15
Combined Chiefs of Staff, 57,
   64, 65
Combined Commanders, 59,
   63, 66
Cork, Freedom of, 2
Cotentin, 57, 60, 65, 66, 70
Cromwell, 47, 56

Cuddesdon, 2, 3, 162, 165
Damaskinos, Archbishop, 134
Davidson, Lord, 142, 145
D-Day planning, vii, 57-76
D-Day resources, 64, 65, 66
de Gaulle, General Charles,
   114
Dieppe, 80, 93
discipline and morale, 87-9
Divisions:
   18th Infantry, 24, 26, 29, 44
   31st Indian Armoured, 114
   43rd Infantry, 85-6
Dombas, 39
Douglas, Marshal of the RAF,
   Lord Sholto, 58
Dovre, 33, 34
Egypt, 103, 104, 120-2
Eighth Army, 52, 68, 97
Eisenhower, General Dwight
   D., 67, 68, 69, 70-1, 96, 98,
   170
Far East, 50, 52
Farouk, King, 104, 120-2
First World War, 6, 7, 8-13,
   162, 165
fishing, 48, 54
Fitzherbert, Major C., 89-91
Free Greek Army Mutiny,
   105, 130-3
Free Greek Navy Mutiny,
   105, 130-1
GHQ BEF, 11, 12, 13
German Army, 49, 66, 87
Germany, 13, 17-22

Geyr, General Baron Leo, von Schweppenburg, 19-22, 24n, 159, 170

Glub Pasha, 106, 139

Greece, 103, 123, 127-36, 158

Greek Sacred Regiment, 134

Green, Richard, 25n

Grigg, Sir James, 68, 93, 96, 97, 106, 159-60

Hay, Ian, 92

Home Forces:
Chief of Staff, 44-56
C.-in-C., 52, 77-93, 158, 166

Home Guard, 45, 47

honours and awards, 9, 12, 14, 15, 46, 53, 105, 123, 134, 135, 136, 150, 155, 158, 165-7

Hore-Belisha, Lord, 21

Horrocks, Lieutenant General Sir Brian, 161

Hotblack, Brigadier F.E., 28, 29

Houldsworth, Brigadier H.W., 92

Humblot, General, 112, 115

Imperial Defence College, 14, 16, 166

Infantry, School of, 86, 87-8

Infantry, status of, 80-2, 83

India, 5, 17

Iraq, 103

Ironside, Field Marshal Lord, 44, 46

Ismay, General Lord, (Pug), 72, 73

Israel, 102-3

Joint Chiefs of Staff, 69

Joint Commanders, 68

Kent-Lemon, Lieutenant Colonel A.I., 31

King's (Liverpool) Regiment, 6

Kirke, General Sir Walter, 44

Kitchener, Field Marshal Lord, 1

Kram, 32, 33

Lebanon, 103

Lee, Major General C.H., 99

Leeper, Sir Reginald, 130, 132-3

Leese, Lieutenant General Sir Oliver, 97, 98

Leigh-Mallory, Air Chief Marshal Sir Trafford, 68, 76n

Leskasjog, 32, 39

Liddell-Hart, Basil, 74

light anti-aircraft battery, 168, 30

Loewen, Major General Charles, 59, 72-4

Loos, Battle of, 8, 9

Lowe, Lieutenant Colonel A., 95

Marshall, General George, 56, 96

Massy, Lieutenant General H.R.S., 26, 38

McCormack, Brigadier P., 104

Middle East Command, 97, 101-26, 166

Middle East Confederacy, 116-18

Miller, Mrs N., 99
Montgomery, Field Marshal Lord Bernard, x, 24n, 51, 52, 67-71, 78, 91, 95-100, 109, 125, 159, 170
Moore, Sir John, ix, 41, 78, 80, 108
Morgan, Lieutenant General Sir Frederick, 57-76, 170
Morgan, Brigadier H. de R., 28, 30-2, 33, 36
Mountbatten, Admiral of the Fleet, Lord Louis, 58, 95

Nahas, Pasha, 126
Nicholson, Lieutenant Colonel C.G.C., 29, 33, 43
Normandy, 57, 59, 60
Norway, vii, 26-43, 49, 166
Norwegian Army, 28, 29, 31, 33, 37, 39
Nye, Lieutenant General Sir Archibald, 99

OVERLORD, x, 7n, 57-76
Overture to Overlord, 57, 76
Oxford, 4, 16, 22, 24n
Oxford, Bishop of, 2, 3
Oxfordshire and Buckinghamshire Light Infantry, ix, x, 7n, 9, 15, 16, 24n, 107, 154, 160, 165, 166
Oxfordshire Light Infantry, 5, 6, 166

Paget, Edward, 2, 7n, 10, 151
Paget family motto (*Labor Ipse Voluptas*), 17, 99, 102, 105

Paget, Francis, 1, 2, 3, 5, 7n
Paget, Helen, 1, 2, 3, 16
Paget, Humphrey, 2, 3, 4, 6, 9, 168
Paget, Sir James, 2, 7n, 17
Paget, Sir John, 12
Paget, Sir Julian, vii, viii, ix, 109, 151
Paget, Luke, 7n
Paget, Tony, 16, 109-11
Paget, Winnie, 12, 111, 152, 165
Palestine, 103, 115, 118-20, 123
Papandreou, Prime Minister, 131, 132
Pascoe, General Sir Robert, ix-x
Persia, 103, 115
Petersfield, 154, 167

QUADRANT, 67
Quetta, 14, 16, 17, 22, 166

Ramsay, Admiral Sir Bertram, 58, 68
RANKIN, 63
Regimental system, 87-9, 162
Reigate, 48
Rhodes, 134, 136
Roosevelt, Franklin D., 57, 58
Royal Air Force, 43n
Royal Engineers, 30, 38
Royal Green Jackets, 9
Royal Hospital, Chelsea, ix, 147-53, 158, 166
Royal Marines, 39, 43
Ruge, General Otto, 28, 33, 34, 37, 38, 42, 43, 171

Sandhurst, 4, 13n, 164, 165
Scobie, Lieutenant General
  Sir Robert, 133, 136
Second World War, 1, 162
Sherwood Foresters, 30
Shrewsbury School, 4, 146,
  158, 160, 165
SICKLE FORCE, 29-43, 164
SKYSCRAPER, 57-76, 97, 167
Smuts, Field Marshal Jan, 106
Smyth, Brigadier H.E.F., 30,
  32
South Eastern Command, 44,
  48-51, 166
St Paul's School, 47
Staff Colleges:
  Camberley, 14, 15, 23, 166
  Minley, 23, 25n, 35, 41
  Quetta, 14, 16, 17, 166
South Rhodesia, 7n
STARKEY, 63
Syria, 103

Tedder, Marshal of the RAF
  Lord William, 69
Tennant, Vice Admiral Sir
  William, 114, 126
Territorial Army, 45

Thomas, Major General, 85
Thompson, R.W., 57, 63, 75,
  91, 171
Thorne, General Sir Andrew,
  98
Trevor Square, 12, 13n
training, vii, 15, 47, 48, 53, 77-
  93
tributes, 125-6, 159-60
Tripolitania, 103, 122

Utterson-Kelso, Major
  General E., 82-3

Verma, 39

War Office, 14, 17-22, 29-43,
  34, 44-5, 52, 166
Wavell, Field Marshal Lord,
  81
welfare, 105, 107, 108, 150
Wellington, Duke of, 41, 78,
  84, 87
Wilson, Field Marshal Lord
  (Jumbo), 97, 98, 130, 133

York, Duke of, 1
York, Duchess of, 1
Yorkshire and Lancashire
  Regiment, 30, 36, 40